Doc

The Legacy of Dr. H. B. Cowart

South Mississippi Country Doctor

(1881-1970)

Jane E. Marshall Brister

EAKIN PRESS ⅦP Fort Worth, Texas
www.EakinPress.com

*A percentage of profit from the sale of the books will be donated
to the Pearl River Community College Foundation.*

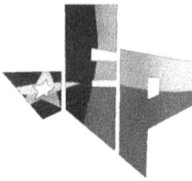

Contents

Acknowledgments

Kathryn Moody has provided invaluable information for much of this book. Our extended families have been inextricably tied since before my birth. That we lived in the same town for many years has added to the worth, dimension, and depth of the stories we have tried to preserve in this book. Being a generation ahead of me, she has brought enormous energy and unparalleled insight to this effort. Thank you, Kathryn.

Kathryn's daughter, Miriam, not only filled in some gaps in our collective memories of Doc but was as much a source of encouragement as Kathryn, through telephone calls and e-mails during the months of research. Without Miriam's input, we would have been searching much longer for the answers.

Kathryn's son, Buddy, provided much needed perspective—a male's view of Doc—based on his close rapport and affection for Doc in my grandfather's later years. His stories helped immensely in defining Doc as we knew him during the Fifties.

It is because of another Cowart descendant, Dick Turner, that a wealth of information is available regarding this family of doctors, thanks to his book, *Once Upon a Country Doctor.* Also an important catalyst in the research phase of Doc's biography were letters from Mrs. Celeste Ward of Silver Creek, Mississippi, and from Ms. Jean S. Hartfield of Carriere, Mississippi, reminding me of passages about Hiram Benjamin in Mr. Turner's dramatization of the early Cowarts.

My cousins, Mrs. Charlene Lane and Mrs. Bill (Marilyn) Sirmon of New Hebron, were very helpful in giving me important information about some of the Cowart family background as well as details about the Johnstons, Doc's wife's family. This information included details of daily life in the early 1900s as they affected the structure of our families. They took me to the Slater cemetery near New Hebron to visit the gravesite of my mother's little brother, James Benjamin Cowart. Charlene also accompanied me to the Monticello cemetery where several Cowart family members are buried. Their support both in local research and long-distance information-gathering gave me valuable insight into these earlier generations of Cowarts.

To the people who so graciously granted me interviews in the fall of 2001 and spring of 2002, I am extremely grateful. Each, in their own way, made an enormous contribution to the development of Doc's personality in a book that could not have been developed without their input. My appreciation for their time and hospitality goes to the following: Ms. Betty Alexander, Mr. J. M. Howard, Jr., Mrs. Rose Lightsey, Mrs. Elizabeth Buckalieu Randle, Mrs. Bonnie Slater Miller, Mrs. Jesse Frances Poole Sandlin, Mr. Sim Poole, Jr., Mr. Benjamin Hiram Slater, Mrs. H. A. (Billie Hunter) Smith, Mr. H. A. (Hack) Smith, Sr., Mr. H. A. Smith, Jr., Mr. Martin Travis Smith, Mr. Leonard Stanford, Dr. W. F. Stringer, and Mrs. L'Rita Rushing Tippy.

For allowing me to quote or paraphrase the thoughtful letters they sent in response to my call for information regarding Doc's practice, I gratefully acknowledge the following people:

Dauenhauer, Anne Davis
Davis, L. M.
DeVries, Ovetta Smith
Edwards, Hazel Stanford
Herrington, Mary Ann
Highstreet, Barbara Gibson
Holston, Virginia (Ginger) Greer
Pritchett, Reba
Riley, Shirley Holcomb

Rouse, Jeannette L.
Seal, Earl
Seal, Margie
Smith, Biser
Stringfellow, Susie
Strahan, Ralph
Thomas, Carole R.
Walley, Lloyd (Mrs.)

A number of people and institutions provided data that gave much-needed background to a story whose main character died over thirty years ago. For their assistance and encouragement during the research phase of this book, I give credit to the following: Bob and Betty Applewhite, Edwin Bass, Dr. Blair E. Batson, John Carney *(Lawrence County Press)*, Jeff and Joy Coker, Ruth Cowart Cole, Dr. John J. Cook, Linda Crawford, Peggy Daniels, Marilyn Dillard (Pearl River Community College), Bess Dillen, Sherry Dixon (The Mississippi Library Commission), Kellie Dooley, Dr. Malcolm Graham, Dr. Patsy Hallman, Joan W. Hartzog (Editor, Cemetery Records of Lawrence County, Mississippi), Trish Johnston, Diane Reese Jones, Senator Trent Lott, Walter Lowe (Historian, Pearl River College), Marie Manor, Dr. Archie McDonald (East Texas Historical Association), Clarice Miller, Todd Moland, Gwen Jenkins Montjoy, Ann Rouse Morris, Winona Jenkins Morris, Mable Reese, Dr. Lee Schultz, Fran Sheridan (Robins Air Force Base, Georgia), Dr. and Mrs. Jack Stanly, Nancianne Suber *(The Clarion-Ledger)*, Butch Weir, (Editor, *The Poplarville Democrat*), Patricia Weir Wilkes, and Dr. Charles Wilson.

Margaret Reed Crosby Memorial Library (Picayune, Mississippi)
Mississippi Department of Archives and History
Nacogdoches Public Library
Poplarville Public Library
Simpson County News
Stephen F. Austin State University Ralph W. Steen Library
University of Southern Mississippi Library, McCain Library and
    Archives

Without the loving support of my family, this book would not have been attempted. To my husband Frank, a special thanks for meticulously checking the text for content and technique and for getting the new printer in the middle of writing the book! To my son, Frank Lutz and and his wife, Melanie, thanks for applauding my efforts and your help with world history events. To Ben and and his wife, Diane, my gratitude for your time on the internet searches, with kudos to Diane for finding the unopened bottle of Hadacol on ebay. To Diane's parents, Lori and Darvin Haupert, thank you for your positive support.

To our grandchildren, Joshua, Jeffrey, Marshall, Ansleigh and Merek, I found great energy from the sparkle in your eyes and the joy you bring to this house.

About the Editor

Carol J. Antill is a native Houstonian who has lived and worked in East Texas and Louisiana most of her life. She obtained the M.A. in English at Stephen F. Austin State University, for which her Civil War novel, *Better Angels*, earned the William R. Johnson award for best thesis in 1996. While working as an administrative assistant for the university, she helped launch the first issue of the SFA History Department internet journal, Clio's Eye, with a two-part series article on the legend of Zorro.

I heard about Carol through good friends in Nacogdoches when I was beginning work on *Doc*. She had recently co-authored the biography of Dr. James Taylor, a Nacogdoches physician, *A Dollar a Mile, Fifty Cents a Gate*. Her organizational ability was invaluable in determining placement of a variety of materials, including transcribed interviews, letters, and photos. She served as an excellent editor and writing consultant through the process of building the manuscript as well as formatting it for the publisher. Thank you, Carol, for a job well done. Doc would have said, "She's a precious little piece of humanity."

Introduction

*That which is, already has been; that which is to be, already is; and God
seeks out what has gone by.*

Ecclesiastes 3:15

He did the best he could with what he had for the time in
which he lived. He was a legend in his own time and for me, he
still is. His doctoring fit the times, spanning the early 1900s
through the 1960s. When he passed away in 1970, he was the
last of a breed of country doctors in South Mississippi, not only
in his town, Poplarville, but in Pearl River County, as well as several surrounding counties. As he ministered to the people of
Poplarville, and in the early days of practice, in Gwinville, New
Hebron, Orvisburg, Sumrall, and other areas, he made indelible
history.

This is the story of my grandfather, Dr. Hiram Benjamin
Cowart, known by most as Doc and by those closest to him as
Bigum. A man of varied tastes, Bigum's passion for raising roses
was eclipsed only by his passion for his calling: using his medical expertise to treat people of all strata of society. He sported
a red rose in the lapel of his tailor-made suits, wore good
cologne, and drove powerful cars when the horse and buggy

were retired. He was also known for his tobacco chewing, with dresser drawers full of Drummond tobacco. His involvement in politics propelled him to the position of staff Colonel for three Mississippi Governors. He was as comfortable rubbing elbows with Mississippi's elite at the Governor's ball as he was having the neighbors over to watch Friday night boxing on television.

In 1881 the Cowarts were already becoming known for having physicians in the family, including several of Doc's uncles, who practiced during the steam-doctor era. From my kinship viewpoint, this same blood running through the Cowart veins manifests itself with a deep yearning for the past. I have certainly developed a new appreciation for history and for the unsung heroes of historical organizations since I began research for this book.

Practicing during the Great Depression, Doc would rely on the Irish spirit he inherited from his mother, which best describes his ability to do much with little, due to the limited facilities and medical knowledge of the time. From the early 1900s well into the 1960s, he gave generously of himself, not counting the cost. He was the real thing—a natural born doctor who responded to his calling with a zeal to serve all kinds of people.

Doc must have known a never-ending satisfaction as he ministered to patients he would know most of their lives, from birth to adulthood. In an era that preceded the MRI generation of technology, his talent for diagnosing and treating patients relied not only on his medical training and knowledge of their family history, but a sixth sense. This remains one of his most memorable traits. Perhaps the secret of this type of doctoring was that he knew his patients well, from their lifestyles to their emotional make-up. He also believed in the curative power of mind over matter.

While gathering the material on this man who has now been gone for more than thirty years, I realized that the span of time during his practice encompasses events that changed this country forever. Yet as two world wars and the Great Depression unfolded, Doc remained a south Mississippi country doctor who began his day a little before 5:00 a.m. and never missed a shave at Mutt Cox's barber shop. From the perspective of the current age of Nasdaq and dot coms, old emotions and memories add a dimension of heightened meaning and fresh connections, especially when profiling the life of one so close to the hearts of so many. People managed to do more than survive during hard times—many lived well, on modest incomes and with modest expectations. Examining Doc's life and livelihood revealed much that has been forgotten about living well in a time of national crises.

In his later years, Doc commented that he had "lived life to the lees." How well this expression fit his lifestyle, that of a man literally on call day and night, in all kinds of weather. During an interview with Junior Howard, a patient of Doc's during the fifties, I said I hoped I could do justice to Doc. He replied spontaneously, "No one could do him complete justice but you can come closer than anyone." I have tried to do just that. From Pearl River County to California, a number of people have made significant contributions toward this endeavor. Through the recollections they shared with me, they helped balance the picture of a man who lived before the issues of stem cell research and DNA manipulation brought such complexity to the domain of the family physician. In the shadow of this new and daunting century, it seems fitting, if not restorative, to return to the past, perhaps to seek a bridge to help us assimilate these complex issues.

Chapter I

Family History

One generation's memories become mists if we don't repeat them and try to remember. It seems so strange that grandchildren's hearing has to wait on a time when they will listen to such. It can happen overnight. Understanding and acceptance are late-blooming twins of young adults' timing.

Kathryn Moody, from The Cowart Album, 1996

In the 30-plus years since my grandfather's death, most of the people who were closest to him in his medical practice, his friends and immediate family, have also passed on. His impact on the communities that make up Pearl River County and surrounding counties spanned the first half of the twentieth century and his story is as much about his commitment to family as it is about his commitment to his patients.

Hiram Benjamin Cowart came from a long line of physicians, beginning with his uncles, Benjamin B. and Eliezer Cowart (see Cowart Family Tree). If there is a patriarchal physician in the family, it is Eliezer, who started a practice before the Civil War. When the Confederacy put out a desperate call for doctors, he entered the war in 1863, soon joined by his teenage brother, Benjamin B., who vowed to follow Eliezer's footsteps in medicine. After the war, Eliezer left the Monticello area to prac-

1

COWART

A Family Tree of 19th and 20th Century Physicians

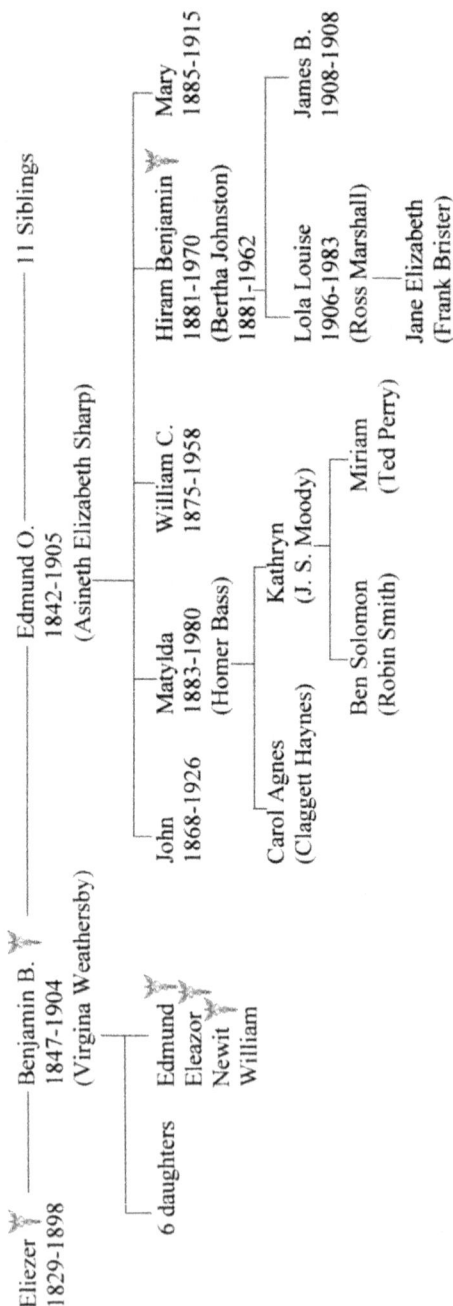

Eliezer
1829-1898

Benjamin B.
1847-1904
(Virgina Weathersby)

Edmund O.
1842-1905
(Asineth Elizabeth Sharp)

11 Siblings

6 daughters

Edmund
Eleazor
Newit
William

John
1868-1926

Carol Agnes
(Claggett Haynes)

Kathryn
(J. S. Moody)

Ben Solomon
(Robin Smith)

Miriam
(Ted Perry)

Matylda
1883-1980
(Homer Bass)

William C.
1875-1958

Hiram Benjamin
1881-1970
(Bertha Johnston)
1881-1962

Lola Louise
1906-1983
(Ross Marshall)

Jane Elizabeth
(Frank Brister)

Mary
1885-1915

James B.
1908-1908

Office of Benjamin B. Cowart, who practiced here in the 1870s.

tice in Fair River, while Ben returned to Monticello and married a local girl named Virginia Weathersby. Benjamin established a practice, taking most of his training from Eliezer, while raising cotton within a few miles of another brother, Edmund O. Cowart, who had served as a nurse during the Civil War but who chose not to pursue medicine when he returned to the Cowart homestead. Though Edmund chose to continue the family livelihood of farming, the Cowart line of physicians did not end with him or his brothers. Three of Benjamin's four sons—Edmund M., Eleazor, and Newit—would later find their niche in medicine. And of course, Edmund O.'s son, Hiram Benjamin, would become the "Doc" who inspired this book.

The last half of the nineteenth century proved to be an era of both hope and despair for the Cowarts, when it came to medicine. One of the greatest medical advances during the Civil War involved the use of anesthesia. Unfortunately, though it may have made surgery a more viable option for those who would have perished without it, its usefulness for the Cowart doctors after the war paled in the face of ravaging diseases like yellow fever, typhoid, pneumonia, and tuberculosis. Effective treatment for these diseases, which tended to be epidemic in character in the humid climate of the South, would not be discovered until most of this generation of Cowarts were gone.

Before antibiotics, penicillin, and quinine, doctors were of an eclectic sort in the South, patterned to some extent in their approach after a farmer who was called Doctor because of the success of his common sense method of treating the life-threatening diseases of the day. Samuel Thomson's theories, among them the steam-bath treatment for pneumonia victims, earned him a following that included Eliezer Cowart. Though Eliezer's application of the Thomsonian method to help his own family was largely unsuccessful, he nevertheless was one of many physicians in the South who subscribed to a practice that earned them a place in history as "steam doctors."

Neither the Cowart doctors nor their families were immune to the illness and death they witnessed in their profession. Benjamin B.'s life was cut tragically short while attending a woman in childbirth. During the woman's long labor, a storm raging outside the patient's cabin caused part of the roof to collapse, dropping a beam on Dr. Cowart and rendering him helpless with internal injuries. Staying conscious long enough to instruct the husband, who helped his wife through the difficult birth, Benjamin did not get help for his own injuries soon enough to stave off pneumonia and died scarcely two weeks later, a month prior to his son Eleazor's graduation from medical school. Perhaps it was fortunate that he did not live to see the death of another son who had chosen the profession. Edmund M., at the age of 38, met a violent end on his way home one night, when two drunks stopped him, engaged him in a fight, and killed him.

The odds seemed to favor the wives of these Cowart doctors, most of who gave birth to several healthy offspring and lived long lives. Eliezer's namesake, Eleazor, married a fragile beauty named Eliza and though he managed to see her through a brush with tuberculosis, the couple lost two of their children, one to scarlet fever, the other to pneumonia.

According to his daughter, Matylda, Edmund O'Neal was an infantryman as well as a nurse during the war, and upon his discharge he was given some papers, a gold coin, and a mule. The mule died before he reached home and Edmund settled on a hill between Monticello and the village on Silver Creek known as the Hall. Recognized for his farming expertise, particularly with orchards and cotton, Edmund was also known as a "scalawag Republican," winning election as a State Representative in 1874. In 1900, there is a public record of Edmund O. Cowart taking the twelfth U.S. census in Lawrence County. Edmund O.'s wife, Asineth Elizabeth, was known as Aunt Sang because she sang very loud and often. Edmund O. had bought her a piano and was forced to move it to the barn when she got too loud with it.

Two brothers, John and William Cullen Cowart, preceded Hiram Benjamin in birth. The older brother, John, and his wife had a son named Max, who worked with the National Red Cross and was overseas during World War II. Doc's younger sister, Mary, married Nick Meriwether, a civil engineer, and lived in north Mississippi, until her death during childbirth in 1915. She is buried in the Cowart Cemetery in Monticello, along with Edmund O. and Asineth and several other family members.

The Edmund O'Neal Cowart Family. L-R: Hiram Benjamin (Doc), William Cullen, Edmund O., Asineth Elizabeth, Mary, Matylda (c. 1890s).

Gravesite of Doc's parents, Edmund O. and Asineth Elizabeth Cowart. Monticello Cemetery, Mississippi.

Matylda Cowart Bass and Doc in the backyard of the house on South St. Charles Street, Poplarville, 1956.

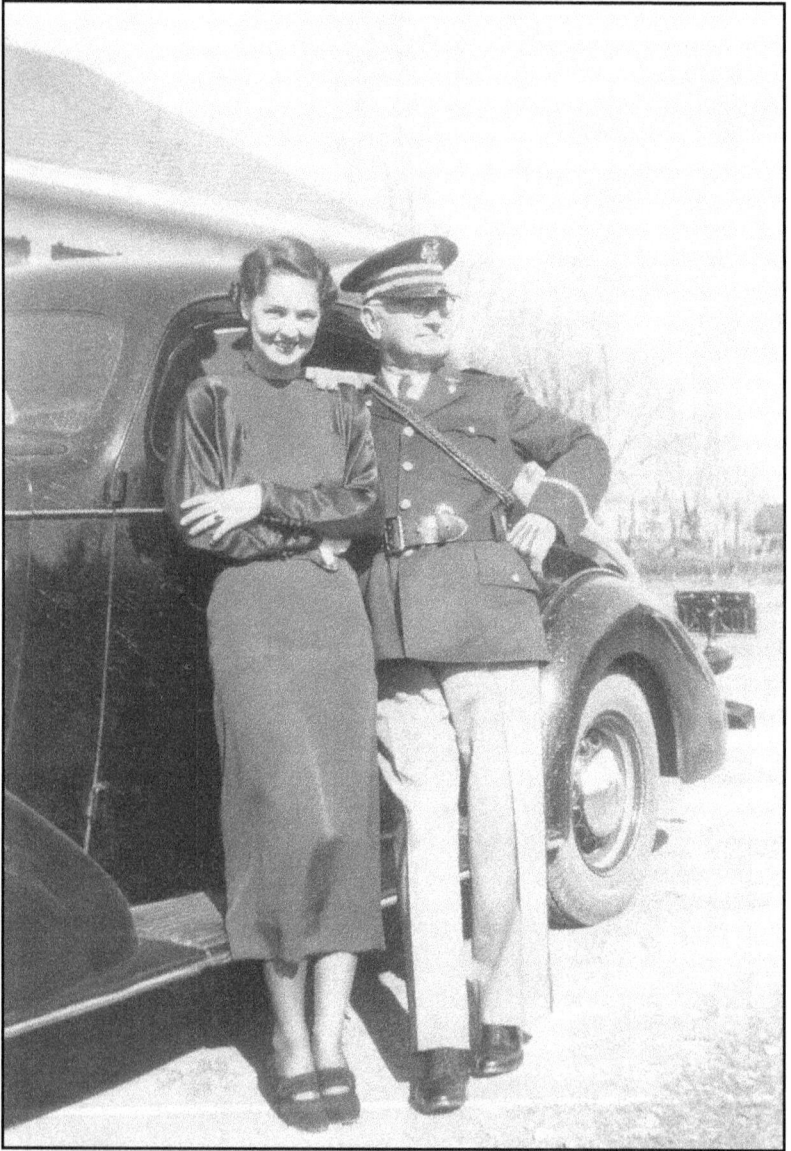

Dr. Cowart and niece, Kathryn Bass Moody, 1934.

Doc's other sister, Matylda, and her husband, Homer Llaron Bass, eventually moved to Poplarville, when Doc was still practicing medicine there. In addition to two daughters, Kathryn and Carol Agnes, they had a son, Homer Llaron Bass, Jr. who was born in 1912 but died of diphtheria as a baby. He is buried in Columbia next to a sister, Martha Eleanor, who was still-born. Kathryn Miriam Bass married J. S. Moody in 1937 and still lives in the family home in Poplarville, where the older Moodys raised J. S., along with ten daughters. Kathryn and J. S. raised a daughter, Miriam, and a son, Ben Solomon Moody (Buddy), a namesake of Hiram Benjamin. Following in the footsteps of his great uncle, Buddy served his country under yet another connection to the medical profession: The war was Vietnam and Buddy, as a medic with the 101st Airborne, received the Bronze Star for his lifesaving actions. Kathryn's sister, Agnes, is an active octogenarian living in Arkansas.

By the time Doc was starting a practice (c. 1905), his uncles had either died or were approaching retirement. Their practices had covered a number of counties in south Mississippi, with a large percentage of their clients tied to the timber industry. Eleazor was the first "company" doctor, building his clientele as an employee of the Inda Pine Company. When he relocated to Capitan in 1908, his younger brother Newit assumed his position with the lumber company. It is highly likely that Doc inherited the majority of his patients from a physician who also happened to be a relative. On January 22, 1915, the *Pearl River Countan,* published in Carriere, reported the following obituary:

> After a long illness and suffering from complicated maladies, Dr. W. F. Spence died at his home Monday evening, January 10th. The news of his death was received with sadness throughout this entire area where he had given his entire professional life to the people. He was 73 years old and had been in the actual practice of medicine for over 50 years . . . For more than a score of years he was the only physician in a wide area.

The day that Dr. Spence died was Hiram Benjamin Cowart's 34th birthday. Though he had not yet moved to Poplarville, Doc was well on his way to building the kind of reputation for which

Dr. Spence was remembered in Pearl River County, that of the country doctor who made long trips in rain, mud, and cold over almost impassable roads to visit the sick, without regard for payment. He went whether those in need were able to pay or not.

In 1881, the year that Hiram Benjamin Cowart was born, the Cowart doctors were well-established in rural Mississippi, tending the families of an agricultural society, from cotton farmers to lumber mill workers. To understand the boy who grew up in this society, I found no better source than the following excerpts of a letter written by his niece, Kathryn Bass Moody:

> This must come from my frame of time that was a part of the whole of my life. I could never think of Dr. Hiram Benjamin Cowart as an individual who was registered in all the right places and who lived and died and never left a track on these corridors of all our lives. In my studied opinion, he was an icon in an illustration of an era. His life and times fit perfectly in the slot of history that they were meant to...rounding out the years of the country doctor who seemed to have risen up out of a typical Mississippi farm family with deep roots in religion, politics, and medicine. It is recorded that there were five doctors in his father's family, all trained at colleges or universities, and all residents of South Mississippi. His mother was a feisty, very small lady who had come to America from Ireland with her family when she was in her teens. She wore a size one and a half shoe and was five feet tall. She and her sister studied what was called a copybook on the boat for their schooling. Doc's father, with his brothers and uncle, migrated to Mississippi from South Carolina and became a successful farmer and livestock owner in the Pearl River bottomland. In hearing my mother, Matylda, who was Dr. Cowart's sister, tell of their growing up, there was always that note of pride in speaking of Ben. In fact, the whole family must have recognized that he had high ambition and resolve, because the whole family did double duty so that he could go to medical school. He continued until his dying day to be generous in his love of family and sharing everything he had to make each relative reach his/her potential.

> But, to put him on paper is like boxing up clouds to mail to the next generation. I do want them to know, but sometimes remembering is so touching that it is hard. Somehow, you want it all back, happening again, so that you can really appreciate it.

His days were surprisingly structured—getting up at five and eating a big breakfast and going to the barber shop for a shave and to decide the current elections and then to the office. No matter that he might have been up all night birthing babies or comforting some very ill patient who only responded to his reassurance. I can still smell the Tichenors' antiseptic cleanness of his offices—one for whites and one for blacks, which was obligatory, but which he never liked and often mixed up on purpose. Somehow, going to his office was never scary, even if it did portend mopping your throat with fire, or giving you a packet of powders (for whatever, it was medicine universal), or talking you out of a disappointment you had imagined, or challenging you to be your best.

He was adamant about every person having a chance for an education, often helping any way he could. He could read his patients like books, often knowing more about their real needs than they. He knew when to honor their pride and take a little money and barter, and he knew when to dismiss the matter of paying until they were ready and able. He took lots of barter. He seemed to be tireless, and always ready to talk. He also listened and became very savvy about state politics, serving on three governors' staffs. He could go to a political rally and make a big difference in the promises the current politicians would make in their speeches. He loved a crowd when there was a cause, no lollygagging, though. He was most comfortable, I think, with his family, at home, sometimes visiting with J. S., whom he adored and who adored him, and watching the boxing matches on T.V. I so well remember when the Pearl Harbor disaster was announced on the radio we were all together visiting at his home. His whole demeanor changed and he began to start brooding about what would come after this. I became very familiar with the deep-seated trait in the Cowart family of deploring injustice. It is not to be stood for, and don't you ever, ever forget it. There was the dark time when his only daughter's little family was torn apart by an affair on the part of the husband. Uncle Ben was pretty hard to restrain from his anger, and I sometimes wonder if he ever got over that. There was so much that went on before, his sending the couple to Columbia University and then to enable the son-in-law to get a higher degree in teaching while Louise stayed home and had their baby daughter. It could not be reconciled in his mind, and the long story of Jane's life began. This would be a good time to say that none of Doc's nobleness or very existence would have been possible without his extraordinary wife and partner, Aunt Bertha. Louise was remarkably loving and caring for all of her life, too. It was so good to know that the final chapter in that story was a wonderful reconciliation of the little original family with the hearty approval of all who were still living then.

My most important personal story is about the birth of our son. After our daughter was born, I had several miscarriages. When Uncle Ben realized how much we wanted another child, he called in a few favors from Oschner's Foundation Hospital, no less. The hospital was just being built, and the Board that governed the Foundation Clinic was made up of five doctors, one of whom Uncle Ben had known since childhood, and to whom he had mentored on several occasions—Dr. Tyrone. Dr. Tyrone became our doctor who successfully helped us through a difficult pregnancy. However, when time came for delivery which we had thought would be at home again, it became apparent that we must get help. So, in the ambulance headed for New Orleans and Oschner's, there was the ambulance driver (a close friend), Uncle Ben and his nurse and J. S. and me. Speed became very important until we came to a railroad crossing in Slidell with a stalled freight train blocking our way. Uncle Ben politely got out of the ambulance and walked up to the engineer's window and asked him if he knew how to deliver a baby. The startled man said "no" and Uncle Ben promptly told him, "then, move this damn train NOW". As we came upon Irish Bayou and things were getting pretty tense inside the ambulance, a chicken truck turned over right ahead of us and scattered chickens all over creation. After cleaning the windshield, we raced to the hospital where we were met by a whole bunch of white coats and people wanting to help. Uncle Ben was indignant when they wouldn't let him go into the delivery room, so, he went anyway. Everything turned out well, and we were so grateful we named the little baby boy Ben Solomon Moody, even over the objection of lots of in-laws who wanted a junior or a III. Days later, when the Moody family was ready to leave the hospital, there was the same ambulance crew that brought us there to take us home. Everybody was in the little room when Dr. Tyrone and his group came in to see us off. One of the doctors asked who our pediatrician was. J. S. looked at him questioningly, saying, "Our what?" The doctor told him "you know, a doctor for the baby". To which J. S. answered that the baby is not sick, why do we need a doctor? Almost helpless sounding, the man responded "for prescribing a formula and directions on shots, etc." J. S. and Uncle Ben told him that we could manage just fine from here on, and thanked them all as J. S. was handed a bottle of sterile water just in case he needed something on the seventy-mile trip home. J. S. assured him that he would stop and get evaporated milk to add and make a bottle. They still speak of us down there with wonder.

In this day and time, we desperately need heroes from the everyday walk. It is easy to acknowledge greatness in retrospect, but, in my opinion, a life as well-lived as was Uncle Ben's should inspire us to gather our little groups around and challenge them to look deep within themselves and open up their lives to the road they should take.

Ben Soloman (Buddy) Moody (left) and his father, J. S. Moody, Poplarville, 1955.

Chapter II

Early Practice

The past is never dead. It's not even past.
William Faulkner, from *Requiem for a Nun*

Well, I can remember he had a horse named Jake and he was black, and he had a rubber tire buggy. And that horse trotted uphill, downhill, all the way. He never changed gaits, and when he'd [Doc] go up to a fella's house, he never hitched him . . . that horse would stay right there 'til he got ready to go.

Mr. Benjamin Slater, 96
Interview, November 15, 2001

Dr. Cowart attended public schools in the Monticello, Mississippi, area and received training from several universities before beginning his practice in the Goss area in Marion County back in the horse and buggy days. In addition to Goss, he practiced in several other areas in the early 1900s, including Newhebron, Sumrall, Gwinville, Orvisburg, and Lumberton, before settling in Poplarville and Pearl River County in 1928. Bertha Johnston came into his life after he had finished medical school and had begun a rural practice. Doc married Bertha on August 15, 1905, and they lived for a short while in Gwinville,

Doc with daughter, Louise (c. 1907).

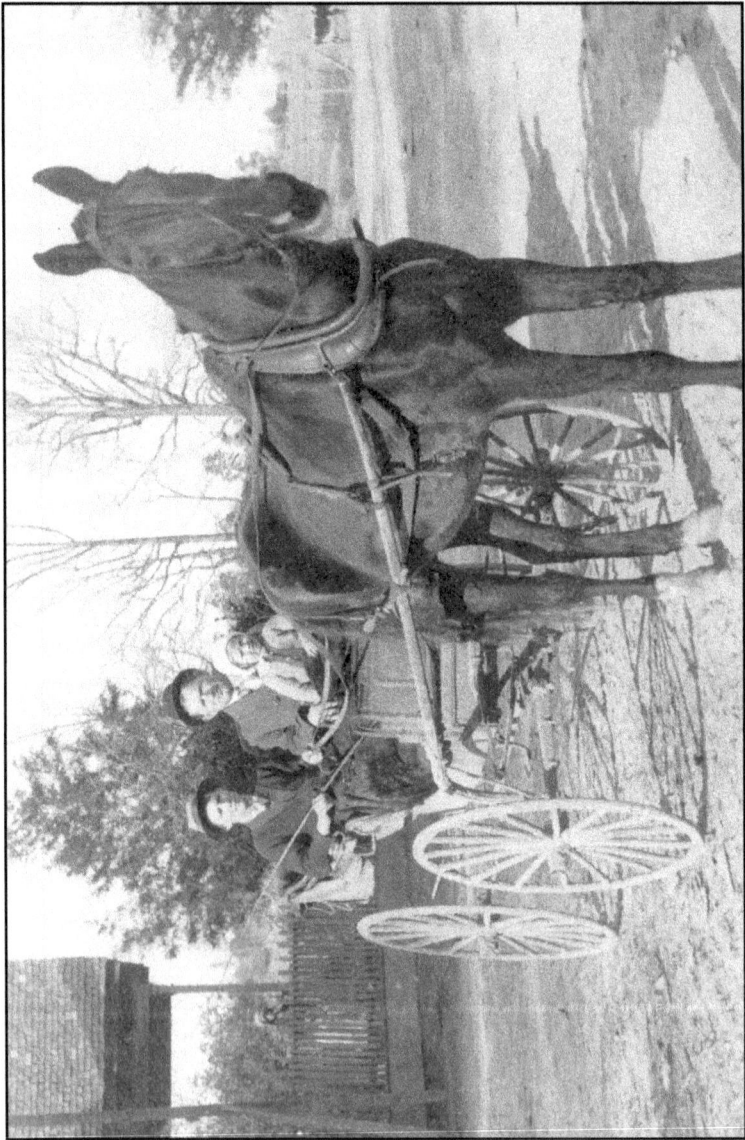

Early medical practice, Jake pulling the buggy. Doc with daughter, Louise, in lap, and unknown driver (c. 1908).

Bertha Johnston and Hiram Benjamin Cowart (c. 1905).

Home of Mr. and Mrs. Jerry Johnston, c. 1905, where Doc and Bertha lived when they first married. Lorraine and Jack Lee standing in front (niece and nephew to Mrs. Cowart).

with her parents, Symira and Jerry Johnston. His father-in-law ran the community dry goods and grocery store, complete with soda fountain. Benjamin Slater remembers visiting that store from the time he was a young boy until it went out of business. The oldest living male child delivered by Dr. Cowart, Mr. Slater was born on December 29, 1905, to Charles Lewis and Pearl Berry Slater in Gwinville. Except for a few years when he lived in Baton Rouge, he has lived on the old home place in Gwinville, which once belonged to his great grandfather. Mr. Slater remembers Jerry Johnston's honor system of extending credit to customers who had little cash, because as a young newlywed, he had to buy on credit. Another vivid memory involves the job he had at the office next to the store, where he helped Doc:

> I washed many a little bottle over there at the store at his office . . . It was just to the right of Cousin Jerry's store—he had a little building to the right of it . . . it was tough. I'd wash 'em, they'd turn them up, they'd drain, then he'd fill them with water, take a teaspoon, take a box of soda, and take a teaspoon, put it in—that's what he would give to little kids with stomach ache.

Newhebron, probably the heart of Doc's early practice when it came to making house calls, was a small but thriving town about 25 miles southwest of Mendenhall, Mississippi. There has been an on-going debate for years—since 1903 by some accounts—about the spelling of the town. Some say it is New Hebron and some say Newhebron. The one-word name remains the official postal designation. In its heyday (1920s-30s), Newhebron bustled, mostly the result of busy cotton gins and a downtown area that featured a hotel, a movie theater and dozens of businesses. These included the F. L. Riley Mercantile Company, the shell of which has an imposing downtown presence to this day. According to the late Charles Little, a retired bank president and community leader, "the town literally had a hum to it, a distinct and musical soundtrack, courtesy of the gin machinery."

Charlene Lane of Newhebron remembers seeing Doc's office in Gwinville. She describes it as having two rooms, un-

Hiram Benjamin Cowart. Graduation picture from medical school, 1906.

Dr. and Mrs. H. B. Cowart, 1906.

painted with one partition. A particularly vivid memory was a jar with a kidney in it (in some kind of preservative) on a shelf in the back room.

Doc received his medical license on November 7, 1906. He attended The University of the South at Sewanee, Tennessee to obtain his prerequisites to enter medical school at the Memphis (Tennessee) Hospital Medical Center, which later was incorporated into The University of Tennessee Medical School. Between 1909-1912, he did graduate work at the Chicago College of Medicine and Surgery (Valparaiso University). In a recent interview with an official at the University of the South, I was reminded that schooling was much different then from the way medical schools operate now, and Doc had to have an equivalent of a teacher's certificate to enter their university. When reminiscing about medical school, Doc said more than once to me that both the University of the South, an Episcopalian institution, and Valparaiso University, a Lutheran school, had a profound effect on him as a young man because of their spiritual atmosphere, particularly the candlelit chapels and quietness that seemed to prevail there.

During the early years of Doc's practice, even a small corner of the world such as southern Mississippi could not escape the diseases that were ravaging Europe. In the spring of 1918, a powerful new enemy emerged, threatening nations on both sides of the conflict known as the War to End Wars. This 'enemy' was a deadly strain of influenza. The Spanish flu, as it was popularly known, hit England and India in May. By the fall, it had spread through Europe, Russia, and Asia, and to the United States. The influenza epidemic killed soldiers and civilians alike. In the end, this global epidemic was more destructive than the war itself, claiming 20 million worldwide. During this pre-antibiotic era, it was no wonder that in the late 1800s and early 1900s, the steam doctors and their theory of botanic medicine, i.e., giving steam baths, eating cayenne pepper, etc., had as much credence as the centuries-old, primitive techniques of blood-letting.

Another disease of epidemic nature, typhoid fever, caused as much fear as influenza when it was diagnosed. During the early years of Doc's practice, the incidence of typhoid was low in

Medical students with Doc (far right) and cadaver (c. 1903).

Young Doc at Hillsdale Lumber Company (c. 1920s).

South Mississippi. However, a house call to treat a child in 1933 resulted in a diagnosis of typhoid, which led to an extraordinary turn of events, as revealed in the following letter:

In February, 1933, I developed a severe frontal headache and persistent high fever. Doc Cowart made a house call. He thought I might have sinusitis. He ruled this out by flushing out my sinuses by squirting a clear fluid from a syringe up my nose. When the return fluid showed no sign of infection, he ruled that diagnosis out. The symptoms continued over the next two to three days. I had no physical signs except the high fever (103-105 degrees). I felt terrible and had no appetite whatsoever. Doc saw me daily. Then he said that it looked like a case of typhoid fever to him but that there had been no cases in the county during the last ten years. He then arranged for Dr. Rouse, a native of Poplarville and a resident physician at Charity Hospital in New Orleans, to draw blood and take it back to New Orleans for culture. Two to three days later, he called Doc—the culture was positive for typhoid organisms. The only treatment then was supportive—keep up my nutrition, maintain good fluid intake and take castor oil for constipation, etc. I was placed on isolation quarantine in my room at home and I was nursed 24 hours a day by a former servant who came back to take care of me. My fever finally broke in about three weeks. I was lucky; I could have died.

The advent of a new case of typhoid fever was like a bombshell in the Health Department. They set about trying to discover how and where I became infected. Everyone who lived or worked in our home had stool cultures—all negative. Water supply (well) and milk (we had our own cows) were tested—all negative. I was questioned repeatedly about creeks or ponds that I might have drunk from. I never did that because my father (who had typhoid fever in his early years) had driven home strongly the fact to my brother and me that it was a dangerous thing to do at the time. It was my impression that my questioners were doubtful of my veracity.

Some months later there came an inquiry from the Health Department on the Gulf Coast. Over the previous two years there had been twelve confirmed cases of typhoid fever scattered along the coast. All investigations for a source were negative and there was no commonality found among these twelve people until that point. Then two new cases occurred, the wife and the son of an oysterman in Biloxi. In addition to tonging oysters in Mississippi

Sound, he peddled his oysters and other seafood from door-to-door a day or two a week locally and in Pearl River County. It was established that the wife, son, and all the twelve typhoid fever patients had eaten raw oysters obtained from the oysterman. Our family had bought seafood from him regularly and had consumed raw oysters also. The circle was closed.

Epilogue: Health authorities had been noting such sporadic cases along all the Gulf Coast States. They were fairly certain that they were being caused by oysters tonged from legally mandated off-limits beds contaminated by the uniform and legal discharge of human sewage into coastal waters. They confiscated a load of oysters from the Biloxi oysterman after they had determined that he was tonging oysters from an off-limits bed between midnight and dawn. These oysters were cultured and one was positive for typhoid. The oysterman was taken to court and convicted and was ordered to pay a fine and to serve time in prison. At sometime during all of this, one of his other children died of typhoid fever. The judge felt justice had been served severely. He ordered the father to be on probation and not have to serve prison time.

> Blair E. Batson, M.D.
> Emeritus Chairman, Department of Pediatrics
> University of Mississippi School of Medicine

The grandson of Ran Batson, a prominent lumber man in South Mississippi during Doc's era of practice, Dr. Blair Batson today credits Dr. Cowart with encouraging him to follow his desire to study medicine. Dr. Batson served on the faculty at Johns Hopkins School of Medicine before returning to Mississippi in 1955 to chair the Department of Pediatrics at the University of Mississippi School of Medicine. In 1997, a new addition to the University Medical Center, the Blair E. Batson Hospital for Children, was so named in his honor.

Bonnie Miller, Benjamin Slater's daughter, proved an invaluable link to those who lived during the early years of Doc's practice. Recently, Bonnie traveled with her father to visit his younger sister, Ellen Daniels, in Jackson, where she asked her aunt what she remembered about Dr. Cowart. Ellen remembers having the flu when she was about 10 years old and developing what was probably rheumatic fever. Dr. Cowart came daily, gave her digitalis and told her to stay in bed for a year. Ellen said that the leaking valve in her heart healed during the year that Doc

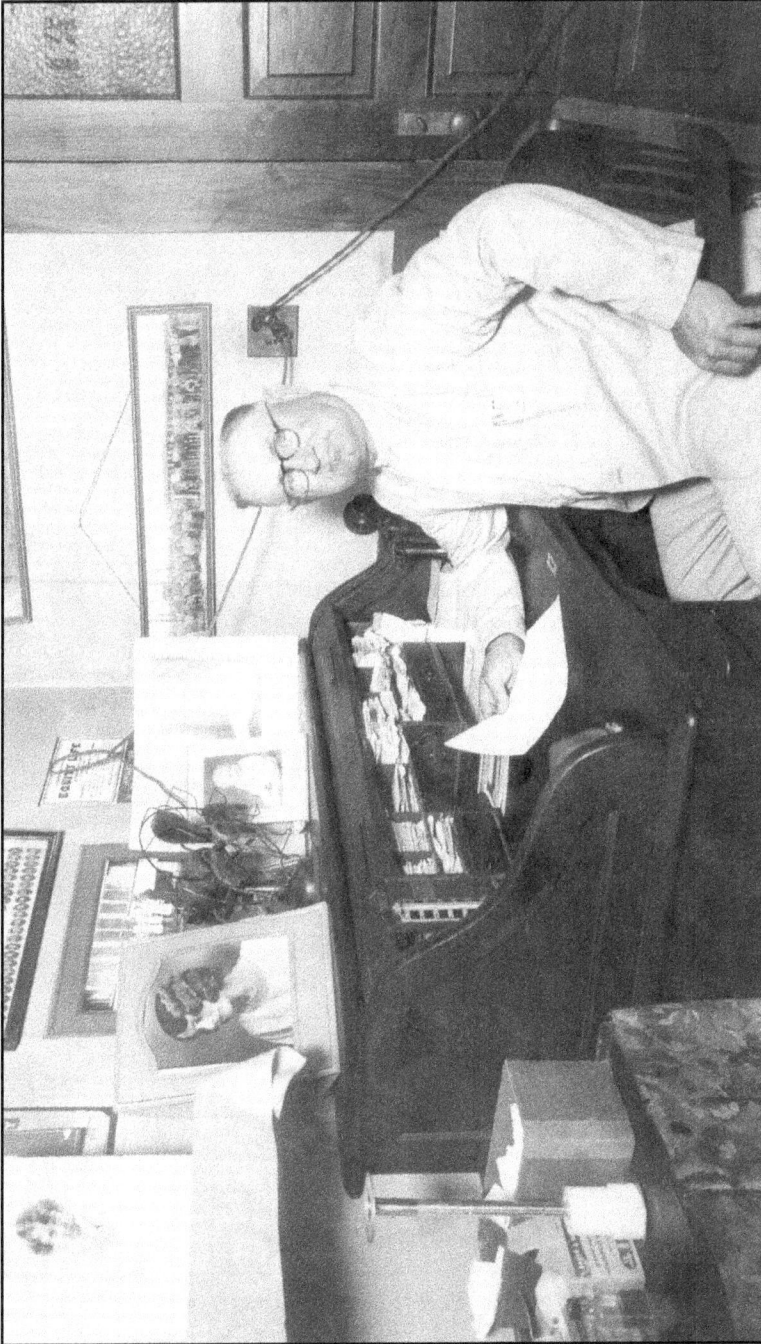

Doc's office in Orvisburg, Mississippi (c. 1920s).

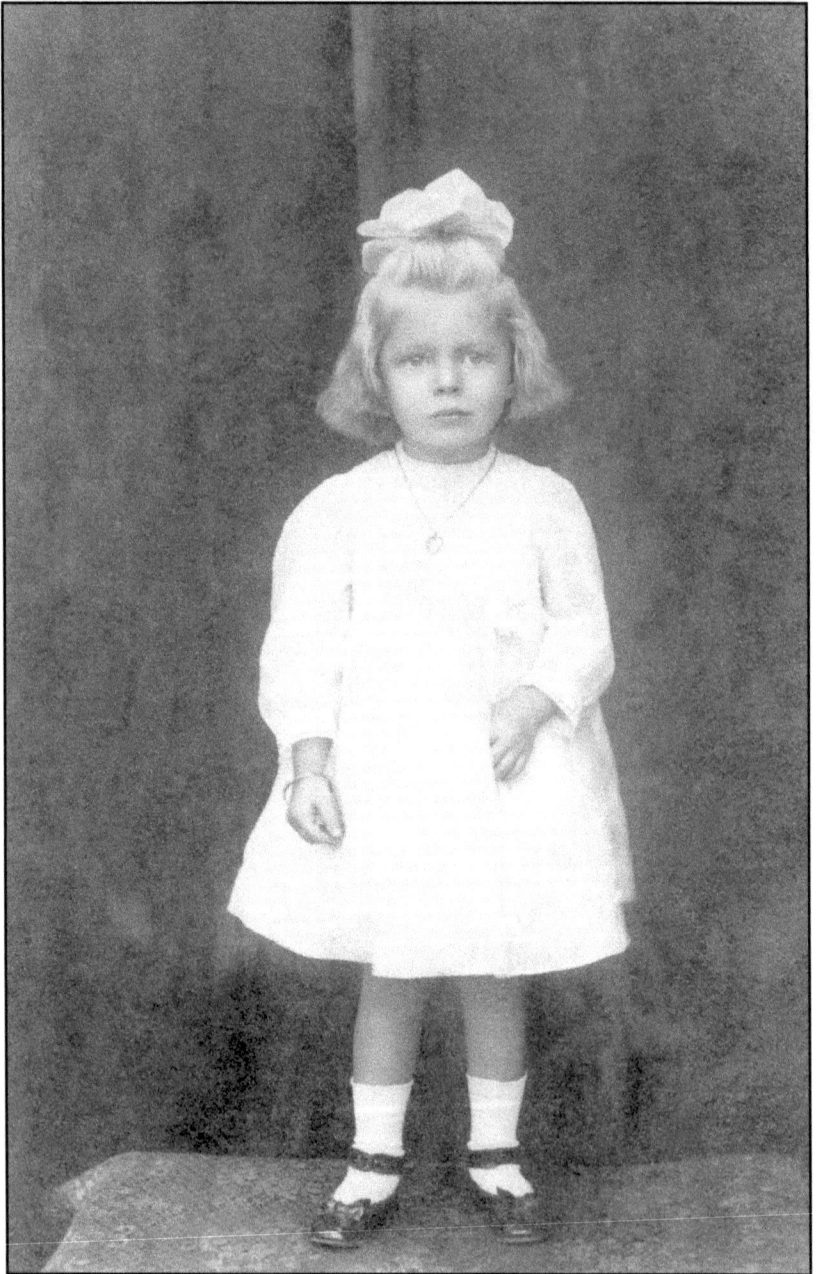

Lola Louise Cowart, daughter of Dr. and Mrs. H. B. Cowart, 1908.

L-R: Lola Louise Cowart, "Sister" Johnston, Betty Sue Berry (c. 1916).

treated her. After she married and was expecting her first child, she wanted to keep Doc as her family physician but he had already set up a practice in Poplarville, and the distance was too great for her to travel at that time.

Benjamin Slater recalls Doc using sheets of cinnamon bark, grated like nutmeg, to flavor his medicine. He describes jugs of medicine sitting on the floor of Doc's Gwinville office, which was small, with a couple of chairs and the examining table. Mercurochrome and other tinctures lined the shelves above the drawers. A number of Doc's former patients still living today remember the iodine-based treatment: cotton on a stick was used to mop throats, and the gagging patient was told not to swallow.

From birth to middle age, Benjamin Slater received the kind of treatment Doc was known for among his patients, most of whom depended on him for several generations. As a young man, he was loading lumber in Shivers, Mississippi, when 160 feet of lumber fell on his hand, pushing the flesh up on one finger. By four o'clock that afternoon, someone had brought him to Doc's office, where Doc pushed the flesh back into place and taped it. Doc routinely changed the dressing for him as it healed. Mr. Slater made blackberry wine with a churn and remembers Doc asking for it on occasion. He would put several gallons of water in the churn, cook the berries, leave them overnight, then squeeze them and strain off the juice. "You'd take two cups of juice and a cup of sugar and put it in there and walk off . . . when it all settled back down to the bottom, you could strain it and you'd have wine."

Apparently, Doc never scoffed at home remedies, and was as likely to acknowledge help from non-scientific sources as from textbook training, as evidenced by the following from Mr. Slater:

> I had to clean one time (I had the flu) and he [Doc] walked to the door and said, "Son, has the flu caught you yet?" He gave me some aspirin tablets and said castor oil and two drops of turpentine would cure most anything . . .

Mr. Slater remembers suffering with malaria one Sunday morning in his bed, when a hornet entered the room and stung him. He had been taking doses of quinine for some time with no abatement of the fever. After the hornet sting, the fever disappeared and never returned. When he told Doc about it, Doc gave full credit to the hornet, perhaps earning him mention as an early proponent of a field of study known as bee venom therapy, which now boasts considerable attention in medical texts. According to a Canadian internet site (www.beelief.com), bee stings have been used for centuries to cure diseases such as arthritis, rheumatism, gout, and other joint-related conditions. The success of bee venom therapy for people suffering from multiple sclerosis, when live bees are applied to areas of the body which have gone numb or become paralyzed, is gaining national attention. The field of apitherapy is widespread in its product base, such as topical lotions and creams containing beehive products such as honey and pollen, and reminds us that the link between ancient remedies and modern therapy can be a revolving door; sometimes the overlooked or forgotten old-time remedies make a significant impact when applied with new technologies.

Payment throughout his service to the people of Mississippi often came in the form of food, which Doc never turned down and usually looked forward to. The usual bounty included fresh garden vegetables, as well as homemade bread and jellies. Doc's niece, Kathryn, who accompanied him on a particular call in the thirties, recalls his sensitivity to the lack of cash among many of his patients:

> I remember once going to the Mennonite colony five miles above town late at night with Doc and his daughter, my cousin, as we were sometimes allowed to do if we did not ask questions . . . It turned out that after a difficult but safe delivery, there were twins. Everything in that home was spotlessly clean and neat. However, there was only one small cradle for the one baby they had expected. Uncle Ben made sure the mother was okay and then turned to take the babies, one at a time, into his arms and put them into the cradle foot-to-foot. Then, he turned to the astounded father and asked for a blanket, which he placed over them to share. They attempted to pay him then and there, as was their custom to pay all debts before sundown. He told them it was good for him to know they were all alright and "he would just

Louise Cowart. College days at Belhaven College. Jackson, Mississipi (c. 1927).

take a couple of those wonderful loaves of bread he kept smelling as they baked".

On March 30, 1950, *The Simpson County News* printed a column by Mr. E. R. Walker, who wrote that aside from Doc's wife, Bertha Johnston Cowart, he probably knew Doc better than anyone:

Dr. Cowart lived and practiced medicine for many years at Gwinville, just over the Simpson county line in Jeff Davis county . . . When we were in knee pants, and about the fourth reader, we lived near Dr. Cowart, and later on lived in the home with him and were closely associated with him for several years. We use to "hitch up" his horse when we had to stand on steps to buckle the collar. The first automobile we ever saw was owned by Dr. Cowart. It had to be pushed through every sand bed, and pulled up every hill. We rode in our first automobile with Dr. Cowart. We drove our first automobile with Dr. Cowart. If all the miles were linked together that we have driven him day and night over the hills and hollows of Mississippi, it would reach around the world more than one time. We will never forget the acts of frightened people and animals as that old Brush car made its way up and down the country. People would line the roads to watch her go by. It was nothing uncommon to see mules and horses running away in the fields with plows and planters as this smoking vehicle made its way down the road. We remember on one occasion two ladies heard the thing coming—you could hear it long before you could see it. They had jumped out of the buggy and were sitting on the fence and the horse and buggy were standing in the middle of the road. We could write a book on our experiences with Dr. Cowart and his first automobile. He has been more than a doctor, he has been a friend and a brother to scores of people throughout Mississippi.

Chapter III

Bigum and Maudie: Life at Home

The heart has reasons which reason knows nothing of.
Blaise Pascal, from *Pensées*

Funny what you remember about growing up. I recall having a lot of fun square dancing on the tennis courts when we would have political rallies and other functions at our Community Center. I'm not sure why we had the square dances on the tennis courts, but they had some good live bands and always had an excellent caller. We wore out the soles of our shoes on those tennis courts. There was a wonderful Methodist minister serving First Methodist Church named Reverend Sells about that time, and he and Doc Cowart were good buddies. Doc told him one time he'd sure rather see me out there dancing than off parked in a car with a boy.

Life at home was occasionally spiced during my teen years with trips to New Orleans. Usually with several girl friends, I would ride the train over Lake Pontchartrain, go shopping on Canal Street and we would not leave until we had sampled the famous New Orleans coffee and checked out all the big department stores: Maison Blanche, Gus Mayer, Godchaux's. We never worried about being in harm's way. Such were the times.

Miriam Moody and Jane Marshall in Cowart backyard, South St. Charles Street (c. 1948).

Jane Marshall Brister and Miriam Moody Perry in Vermont (c. 2000).

Maudie in Cowart backyard with Jane and Miriam on slide (c. 1942).

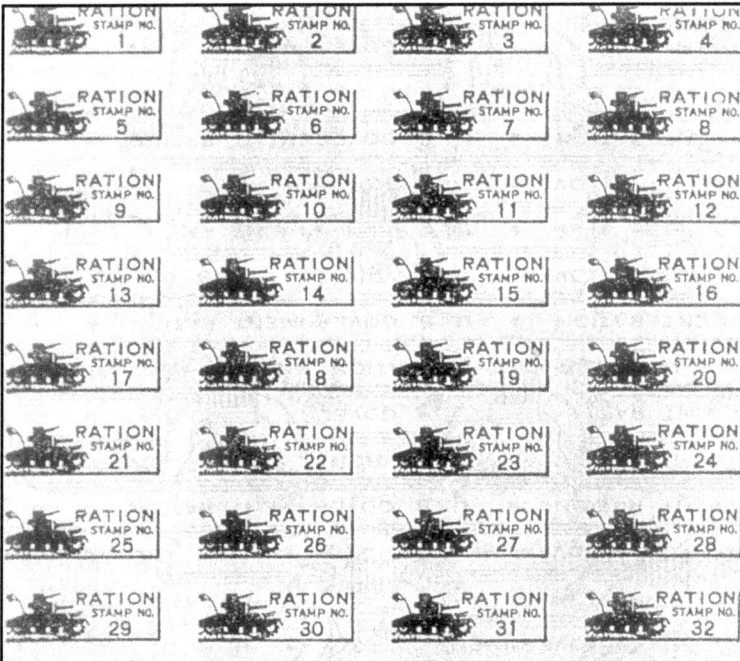

War ration book and stamps, used during WWII.

Author with parents Louise and Ross Marshall, Cowart backyard, Poplarville, Mississippi, 1938.

Doc and author in yard at Cowart house (c. 1939).

For me and a group of close friends, sixteen was the magic age for the stage of "daring-do" in our lives. Under the tutelage of the best of piano teachers, including Miss Sophronia Hyde and Miss Anna Wallace, we had heretofore peaked in playing piano. Writing movie scripts, driving an automobile (at least a Henry J car), acting in school plays, and excelling academically rounded out our need to perform. We were ready for a musical group. With two of us playing ukeleles, we harmonized to the latest ballads. Since there were six of us, we called ourselves the Sixteens. Looking back, the spirit of our group was a reflection of the emotional high that came in the post-World War II years. We were good enough to be invited to a New Orleans TV station, WDSU, to introduce Poplarville—with all its opportunities—to what we thought was the world. We also had air time on WLBT in Jackson, Mississippi. Doc seemed so proud of our boldness, as were all the parents. Somehow, I think that sort of thing disappeared from our society about the same time Bigum left this world.

As a child, I felt totally confident about life with my grandfather. I attended school in Poplarville from kindergarten through not only twelfth grade but my freshman year of college at Pearl River Community College. Homework and piano lessons were routine but never boring, so absorbed was I in a lifestyle that was almost idyllic by some standards of the time.

One of my earliest memories in the house on South St. Charles Street is the clean, fresh knotty-pine smell of the upstairs chifferobes—a popular piece of furniture that served as a closet in homes that were built before the era of subdivisions and cookie-cutter floor plans. The country was not only at war but still digging out of the Great Depression and my parents lived in an apartment above the house my grandparents had bought and remodeled. The upstairs was large and roomy for each of the two bedrooms. In later childhood years, I liked looking out the windows from these rooms because I could see almost all of the neighboring houses from this vantage point.

I could not have been more than eight but I remember my mother using a ration book at the grocery store, and turning out lights to cooperate with blackouts. But in hindsight, our home was a model of order, thanks in large part to the loving partnership of the two people I knew as Bigum and Maudie. Bigum was surrounded by women in his home, especially following my father's sudden departure.

Before I was born, my parents lived in New York, where my father earned a Master's Degree from Columbia University. Times were hard so Ross and Louise Marshall moved in with my grandparents while Ross scouted for teaching positions. Ross taught advanced math at Savannah Public School and later taught several subjects at Pearl River Community College. After I was born, my mother stayed at home while Ross studied one summer at George Peabody Teachers' College, where he became involved with another woman. At some point, Bigum discovered that Ross had a separate mailbox and received mail from this other woman. There was an ongoing personality conflict between Ross and my grandfather, but this discovery ignited the conflict into a full-blown war that culminated in my grandfather literally running Ross out of town. My father moved away and eventually married in another state, while my mother remained with her parents. Until I was in college, I had no word of him and rarely wondered about him. The father image had already been replaced by that of the very strong presence of my grandfather.

The Women's Touch

Between Maudie and my mother, the house on South St. Charles was a haven for Bigum. Maudie planned all the household activities: Washing was on Monday, ironing on Tuesday and a lot of cooking every day. The menu was a big, well-planned item, and fortunately we had plenty of household help. Ellen, our cook, came each day to prepare the noon meal. Bigum rose before five every morning and Maudie put before him a breakfast that included bacon or sausage, eggs, biscuits and all the southern trimmings. Before we had a washing machine, there were two large tubs for washing and rinsing, and a washboard for scrubbing the clothes. Ella Byrd helped with the washing and ironing. My mother, always a quiet, subtle presence, seemed to take great pleasure in hanging clothes on the clothesline.

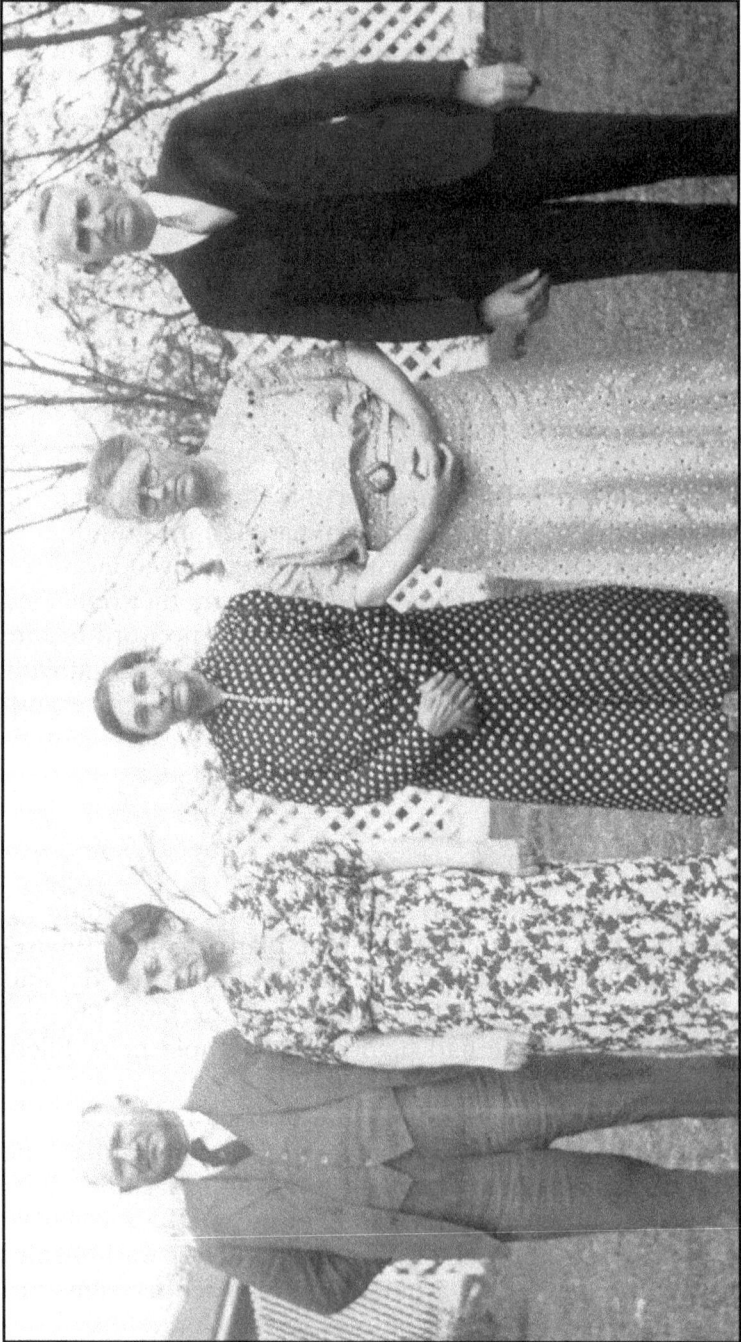

L-R: Doc, Maudie, Hilda Lee (Maudie's sister), Lillie and Carl Johnston (Maudie's brother). Poplarville (c. 1940s).

Author's husband, Frank Brister, and Maudie at dinette table in Poplarville, 1962. Frank enjoyed Maudie's homemade vegetable soup.

Tommie Massey and Doc. Tommie, a cousin on Maudie's side, was referred to as my other mother after my mother and grandmother passed away. Laurel, Mississippi (c. 1950s).

When Maudie's family came to visit, we always had a good time. L-R: (Back row) Hilda Lee, Haskell Massey, Charlene Lane, Dorothy Little, Tommie Massey, Noel Lane, Doc, Mary Hilda Lane. (Front row) Barney Lane, Mrs. Nannie Singletary, Jane Marshall, Marilyn Lane (c. 1947).

Maudie and Louise, my mother, took me to Fines' Department Store in Hattiesburg periodically, so that I would have the proper things to wear. Maudie was always taking care of the details of running a house and home, seeing that clothes were in order for everyone. Several pictures from my childhood show me dressed in a little nurse's uniform, indicating one of the many ways Bigum and Maudie doted on their only grandchild. While Bigum had his pet names for me, Maudie called me her "Angel Child."

Newspapers were vital to Bigum's routine; *The Weekly Democrat, The Clarion-Ledger, The Hattiesburg American,* and *The Times-Picayune* kept him abreast of national as well as local news, feeding his fascination with politics while sharpening a wit that won him friends at many levels—from lawyers to barbers. Since the papers came at different times, some in the morning and others in the evening, I was given the chore of picking them up from the front door or the sidewalk, but still, I liked hearing Bigum call me by a pet name, "Lizabeth" (accent on the 'beth') when he wanted me to get one for him. My names came from both great-grandmothers: Jane for Maudie's mother, and Elizabeth for Bigum's.

The House on South St. Charles

Maudie was as much an individual as Bigum, as conservative as he was liberal on a number of issues. In hearing her tell about remodeling and expanding the Cowart home, she did about as much work and drove as many nails as the carpenter did. The house on South St. Charles Street was a large white two-story structure with dark green shutters—a stately, handsome home that bore witness to Poplarville's greatest period of expansion and most of Bigum's professional life. My grandparents had given me a large bedroom with a walk-in closet at the front of the house. Maudie's touch—a collection of pretty figurines and a chiming clock—adorned the mantle in this room, which afforded me the best view from the house, with two windows overlooking the front porch. Time found expression in almost every room of the house, from the soft chimes of the grandmother clock on the wall next to the TV to the clock on the mantle in the large room that was the center of activity in the house. Due to his long hours, this was also Bigum's bedroom, when it wasn't being used as the sitting room for the family and friends. Three rocking chairs and a lounge chair rounded out the room where Bigum propped up on a mahogany four-poster bed to read his papers beneath a large, swing-over fluorescent light. The walk-in closet in this room housed an old trunk and shelves, where my mother kept dust cloths, furniture polish and stored things.

Then there was the kitchen, the pantry and the area near the back door where there was ample room for the long deep freeze. There was a dinette table with chairs in the kitchen and, in later years, a washing machine in the pantry. Adjacent to the kitchen, a mahogany table and chairs graced the formal dining room, along with a china cabinet and buffet. The living room was open and next to the dining room with several chairs and a mantle with a gas heater in the fireplace, just like all the fireplaces. While Karastan area rugs protected the hardwood floors in these rooms, rugs of various shapes and colors were like islands throughout the rest of the house. We used to laugh about how many doors each room ended up having after the remodeling and expansion. The sleeping porch at the back which joined the room with the freezer had about eight windows, two iron beds and an old fashioned dresser with a tall mirror. Just inside the back door, there was a hallway which led to the stairs to the second story apartment.

In our backyard, Maudie had a stone wishing well built, complete with a roof and trim. Of course, it wasn't a real well, but unless you looked down inside, it would fool anyone and was quite an impressive structure. Next to the backyard, there was a long vacant lot full of rose bushes. On the other side of the house and backyard we had a swing house. Sweetheart roses bloomed next to the swing house, producing a heavenly scent. Behind the two-car garage, there were two separate rooms, one used for washing clothes, the other for smoking meat.

Many summer evenings, Maudie and I would sit on the long, screened front porch listening to the baseball games at the Community Center, which was about a block away. Sounds of

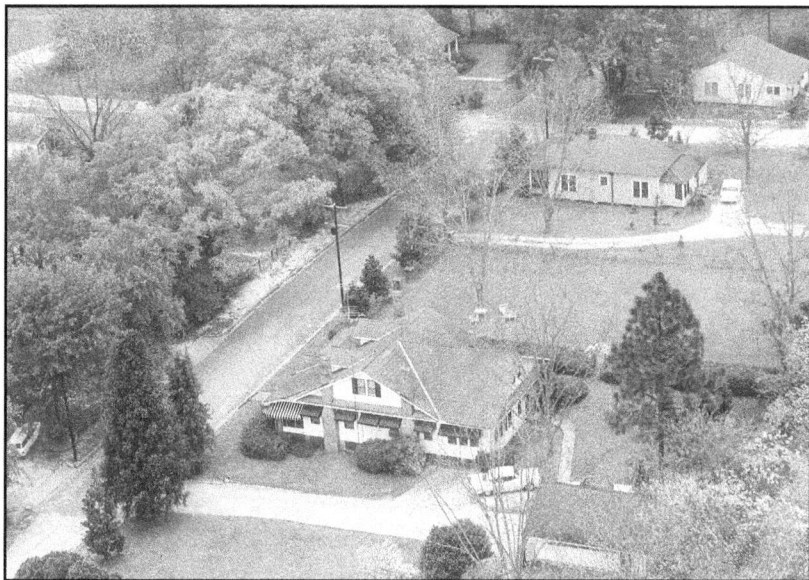

Aerial view of Cowart residence, South St. Charles Street, Poplarville, Mississippi (c. 1950s).

View of Cowart home from street. The house burned down in 1998.

the game, as well as the announcer's voice, came to us clearly in that thick night air and though I thrilled to the excitement of the games, I liked the quiet as well. A feeling of wellbeing—of confidence—emanated from that porch, especially when it rained on the awnings.

The house I lived in with my mother and grandparents on South St. Charles Street in Poplarville no longer stands, destroyed by fire in 1998. Memories of the events surrounding our lives in that home during the 1940s and 1950s are preserved in photos, including a remarkable aerial photo taken in 1960. During the 1970s, a fellow teacher at Brownwood Junior High School in Brownwood, Texas, Ms. Fran Armstrong, painted a watercolor of the house. This framed treasure is currently hanging in my living room.

Guests at All Hours

When people needed a doctor in the "wee" hours, they came to the house. The doorbell would ring in the back room, which we called the sleeping porch, where my mother slept. As shrill as a fire alarm, it woke the entire household. No matter when they came, Bigum took care of the unexpected visitors, sometimes with a prescription and always with words of comfort. He saw about as many patients on the front porch or in the living room as in his office. Some of their illnesses distressed me, listening to them from my bedroom, but most of the time this anxiety was temporary, because Bigum's treatment, even if it was just advice, usually sent them away in better spirits. His emotional base was well-covered in our home, thanks to Maudie. People were welcome all the time and there was much warmth and openness for anyone who came to see us.

Aromas

Christmas brings to mind one of several distinct aromas associated with the house on South St. Charles and Bigum: bourbon-soaked fruitcake. Dr. J. B. Davis of Poplarville, who

Doc in linen suit and Panama hat, Cowart backyard (c. 1945).

worked closely with Bigum, sent over fruitcakes his wife had baked, at Bigum's request. Dr. Davis' daughter, Anne Davis Dauerhauer, remembers the scent of these fruitcakes as her mother baked them; we recall an overwhelming sweetness in our dining room as Maudie kept the fruitcakes wrapped in bourbon-soaked cloths provided by Mrs. Davis. A next-door neighbor in those days, as well as a friend and classmate, L'Rita Rushing, remembers the smell of Maudie's pound cakes when she would come to visit. Everyone loved her pound cakes, especially for dunking in a cup of coffee. As we said back then, it was good eatin'.

Bigum's dresser was covered with two particular gifts at Christmas: Drummond tobacco and cologne. Bigum's patients were generous when it came to supplying him with tobacco, evidenced by the stacks on and in that dresser. Kathryn Moody remembers Doc saying that he started chewing tobacco in medical school to ease the tension when studying operating room procedure. The aroma of the tobacco was present but soon overpowered by the Pine Sol that Maudie used to regularly mop around his spittoon, which she called his enamel slop jar. His office boasted a beautiful brass spittoon, given to him by Mr. Ran Batson of Hillsdale.

An entirely different scent defined Bigum's presence in his use of cologne, or toilet water, as we called it. His preference for one brand of tobacco was echoed in his careful selection of colognes, which were strong but clean. Dr. Titchenor's antiseptic was another scent that many people still associate with him, as he believed in its use as a mouthwash as well as for disinfecting his office.

Details carried as much weight with Bigum as the whole picture. His penchant for pinning a rosebud in his lapel could be traced to a passion for rose bushes that prompted him to travel as far as Tyler, Texas for many of the varieties planted in the lot adjacent to the house. No matter how busy life became, he took great pleasure in walking among the crimson blooms which made an unforgettable picture against the white wooden fence bordering the lot. The essence of these as well as the blooming camellias and Formosa azaleas in our yard was one of nature's gifts he never tired of nurturing.

The rosebud in his lapel was only one of the details Bigum exacted about his appearance. His niece, Kathryn, remembers his flair for suits: "Uncle Ben always wore a linen or a seersucker suit until time for worsted woolen. His hat was always a Panama straw. His shirts were starched and ironed, and his ties were legendary." My mother bought most of his shirts in New Orleans at Maison Blanche or Gus Mayer, always white, which we starched on ironing day. Bigum made many trips to New Orleans, always bringing back something we found exciting. Often, it was the best sugar cane, but he also knew just the clothes to bring home. He did not use canes until later in life, when he actually leaned on them, but probably one of the first ones given to him came from Lt. Governor Carroll Gartin. His collection of canes included one the Mennonites gave him in barter, a cane with the seal of the Mississippi School Supply Company, and one from the Ozark Mountains of Arkansas; often in later years, he carried one that Kathryn's husband, J. S. Moody, brought him from a Jaycee convention in Dallas, an unusual wooden cane with a snake carved around it.

The Lady and the Liberal

Teamwork in our household was amazing, considering the personality differences between my grandparents. Where Maudie was methodical and held to very staunch beliefs, Bigum was impatient and liberal. He definitely liked things his way. Everyone knew what Bigum expected without any special demands on his part. Home was a haven for him and rarely did he mention his patients' problems. When he drove up the long driveway in the evening coming home from a long day, his car roared. Sometimes when he would back out from the garage, in turning the car around to face the street, he would hit the side of the house, leaving a perpetual dent in the wall by the sleeping porch. The drop-off from the driveway to the street was quite steep and often his car would scrape the concrete. I guess no one ever mentioned this to him. We just accepted this as part of everyday life. He was very protective of my mother and me, but this attitude did not come across in an authoritative way. Actually, we knew his mannerisms indicated that he wanted us to be safe and secure and out of harm's way.

He accepted flaws and habits in people and rarely treated his patients with advice that went against their lifestyle, but was quick to point out an injustice. Bigum's multifaceted personality helped him relate to many types of people about almost any topic, no matter what their station in life might be. It seemed to me that he was genuinely interested in each one as an individual. He accepted people as they were without trying to change them. I guess the closest he came to changing a patient's habits came in the way of advice, for example, about not eating fried foods for some stomach ailments or other words of advice relating to some life-threatening illnesses. But to advise patients to change their lifestyles in general wasn't his style. He hoped that I would become a lab technician, saying that it was one of the "prettiest" works one could do, making a significant contribution to humanity. But he didn't push it or try to make me feel guilty in any way when I chose an educational field. He let people be themselves. His strategy was being himself, and he was a natural. He touched his patients' hearts and souls and endeared himself to them. They trusted him. Many times people would come to him for advice and he took on the role of a counselor. Once, a woman came to him, distraught beyond words because her daughter was marrying a Catholic. Back in those days, this was considered unacceptable by many, if not scandalous. I'll never forget his independent and unbiased spirit coming through when he replied to the woman, "Well, Mrs.—, the Catholics might have something to say about that, too."

Bigum and Maudie disagreed about a number of things, but always with respect for each other. We had a good friend who was widowed. When Maudie found out the lady was drinking beer on occasion, she thought this was terrible, even worse than smoking. Much to Maudie's chagrin, Bigum responded to this one day when the subject came up at home. "She's over there all alone—let her have her beer." Neither one changed their thinking but they were free to express themselves, nevertheless.

Doing "The Hadacol Boogie"

Ironically, when I was about 12 years old, my tee-totaler grandmother decided that Hadacol would be a good tonic for me. While I suspect Bigum was laughing up his sleeve, he never said a word. A popular vitamin-mineral medicine in the early fifties, Hadacol was also 11 percent alcohol. A Cajun entrepreneur, Coozan Dudley LeBlanc, developed and promoted the elixir so successfully that a song was written about it. Bill Nettles wrote and recorded "The Hadacol Boogie," a crowd-pleaser in most of the south during the fifties. The song had several verses, which changed slightly with each performer, but a couple of the original verses were as follows:

If your radiator leaks and your motor stands still
Give her Hadacol and watch 'er boogie up the hill;
She'll do—

Refrain:
The Hadacol Boogie
The Hadacol Boogie
The Hadacol Boogie
Makes you boogie-woogie all the time.

The rooster and the hen, they were standin' in the shade
The rooster done the boogie, while the hen laid the egg;
He done—

Refrain

Maudie's philosophy often spilled out in her use of proverbs. A fair-minded lady, she often said, "circumstances alter cases." She was a devout Christian who imparted lifetime values to me without trying. She lived it. I believe she would have been an excellent judge because she was compassionate, yet viewed much of life with impartiality.

I must have been about ten or twelve when some of us girls learned the word "darn." We were smitten with our new word, saying darn this and darn that. One day, Bigum heard our silly new games and he pulled me aside and said, "The word is

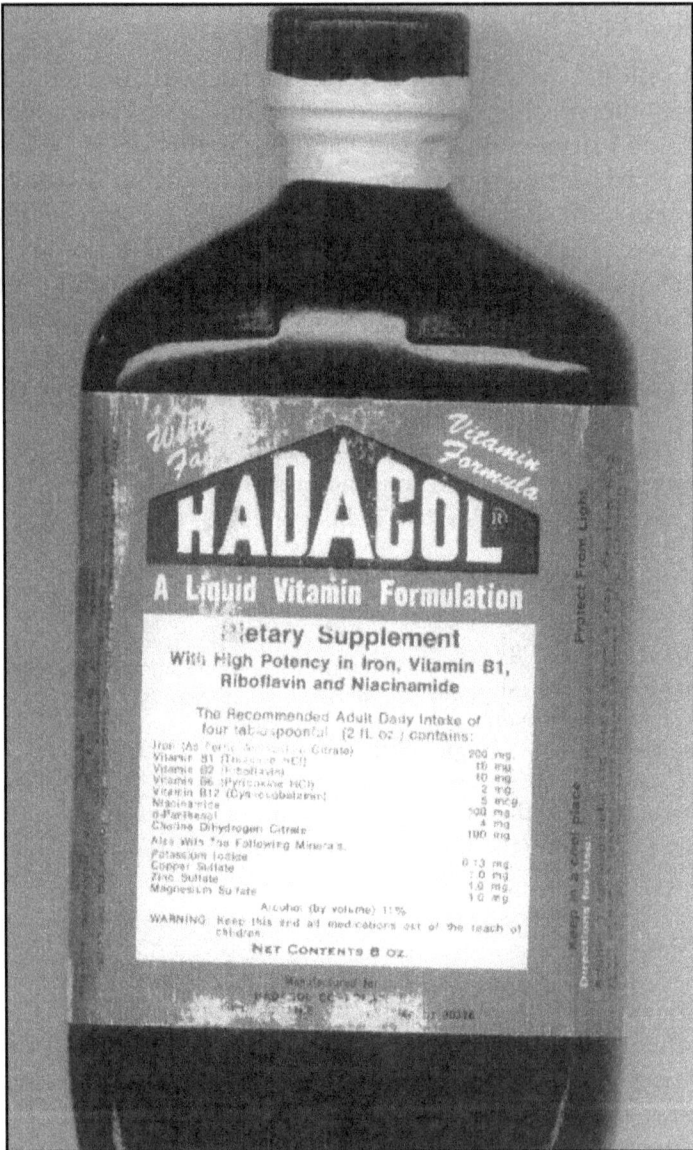

Hadacol, Maudie's elixir of choice when the author needed a vitamin boost, was so popular in the South, a song was written about it.

damn." Imagine my shock at hearing this. I'm sure he knew I would never go around saying damn. But, as in other situations, he tried to break me into the reality of life in general. Funny, when I had permission, I didn't feel the license to take advantage of this new-found expression.

My cousin Miriam and I were caught in the middle of one of the duels between the conservative Maudie and liberal Bigum. We wanted to take ballet and tap lessons, which Maudie opposed because of the short dance costumes that she said were just too ridiculous to wear out in public. When Bigum found out about our desire to dance, he simply signed both of us up for lessons with Miss Dot Beach. From a tap duet to "Deep in the Heart of Texas" to a ballet choreographed to "Night and Day," we loved every minute of the years we had in dance. Many years later, I realized how Bigum saved me from a conservatism that would have closed me off to some of the more beautiful moments in my life.

These lessons learned in retrospect are priceless. And the definitions of the terms, "conservative"and "liberal" have broadened considerably since my childhood.

Show of Shows

When television came into our house, new traditions followed. From one of my interviews with my cousin, Buddy Moody, I gained an interesting perspective for a generation just coming into their own in the late 1950s. He and his father, J. S., were frequent visitors at our house, especially when the men gathered for television boxing. He recalls that the women would evacuate the TV room and would never come back after the boxing started. The porcelain bucket by Doc's bed filled with Pine Sol, which, as he says, appeared to him like "a bucket filled with white water for him to spit in." Many times Mr. Ernest Etheridge, a good friend, and Mr. Ralph Rushing, an extraordinary pharmacist as well as a friend, were present for the boxing episodes.

"Your Show of Shows," "The Hit Parade," and "The Lawrence Welk Show" were some of our favorites. Particularly

L-R: Louise Cowart Marshall, Dr. H. B. and Mrs. Cowart, Jane Marshall, 1958.

impressed by Imogene Coco, Bigum took sheer delight in her performances, claiming she was particularly gifted in being hilarious with the greatest of ease. He couldn't wait for the Lennon Sisters to appear on "The Lawrence Welk Show," and remarked how little Janet seemed to always have a mischievous spark in her eyes; he bet she could get into a lot of "devilment". About five years ago, my husband and I saw the Lennon Sisters perform in Branson, Missouri, at the Lawrence Welk Theatre, where I had an opportunity to tell Janet what Bigum had said about her so many years before. She laughed, saying that she had mellowed some since her childhood years.

Music of the Forties and Fifties entertained our entire family; there was no generation gap when it came to what was played on television or the radio in our house. "The Perry Como Show," Bing Crosby's version of "White Christmas," the Ink Spots' "To Each His Own" and Johnny Ray's "Walking My Baby Back Home" drew us together. Bigum's preference in music was that it have heart. I think he enjoyed Irving Berlin's music for this quality. Comedy was as important as music; many evenings he would sit on the side of the bed watching "The Three Stooges" and literally fall over laughing. I'm sure this was therapeutic for him, a distraction from the illness and death that often dominated a long day of house calls.

If Bigum were around today, I think he would like an album called "Moonlight Becomes You." Of these old favorites recorded by Willie Nelson, he would especially enjoy "You Just Can't Play a Sad Song on a Banjo." I feel blessed to be able to enjoy a wide spectrum of the performing arts, much of which I credit to the exposure to them in my early childhood. On occasion when I went with Bigum on a call, he would turn on the radio and tune in to some "fiddlin'." I think he wanted me to be aware that, while Bach, Listz, and Mozart played an important part in my introduction to the world of music, they were not the only forms of music to understand and enjoy. We had fun and I always felt special to him; the rich residue of those experiences remains deep within me. His rollicking sense of humor still catches me like a net; he knew that a good laugh was the only remedy for some ailments.

Doc, Poplarville, Mississippi (c 1936).

Chapter IV

Life at the Office

The high destiny of the individual is to serve rather than to rule.
Albert Einstein

I'm not sure I remember my first visit to Dr. H. B. Cowart in Poplarville. There were many visits, and they all just blend together. His office was in the Masonic building on Main Street and consisted of a waiting room and his office. As I think back, it seems like I was sick a lot as a child. I remember he always listened to my breathing and looked down my throat.

I only remember one kind of medicine. It was pink powder that came in a paper envelope like a B.C. headache powder. Regardless of where I hurt or was sick, I got pink powder. I might have a sore throat, a stomach ache, or a cut foot. I got pink powder.

Then there were the shots! It seems to me now that I could not walk without stepping on a nail. It is hard for me to remember a time I didn't have a rag with kerosene on it tied around one foot. This was the usual treatment, along with a visit to Dr. Cowart to get a shot to keep me from getting lock jaw. I look at my feet today and wonder how there is anything left to walk on. Besides stepping on nails, there was the time I sawed into my foot while sawing a limb off a tree where I was building a tree house, the time I chopped through a board with an axe and into my foot, and the time I threw a homemade hunting knife and stuck it in the top of my foot.

Back to the shots. The syringe and needle used by Dr. Cowart was far different than those used today. The syringe was stainless steel and glass, about the size of a roll of quarters with a needle on one end and a plunger on the other. The needle was much larger than those used today. The syringe and needles were kept in a solution of chemicals. I knew what was coming when Dr. Cowart took the syringe and needle out of the jar of chemicals. Believe me it hurt!

I remember I was afraid of Dr. Cowart and never wanted to go to his office, but I also remember he was gentle and kind to me. I remember Dr. Cowart as the kind of doctor portrayed in the famous painting of Norman Rockwell showing the boy in the doctor's office.

From "A Visit to the Doctor"
Growing Up Country
L. M. Davis, Chief of Police (Retired)
Lumberton, Mississippi)

For almost forty years, Doc rented the office on Main Street. There was a steady stream of patients coming and going. There was no bookkeeper or receptionist—just Doc and the nurse. I remember when his office visit fee went from $1.00 to $2.00, but I'm not sure of the year. Many times people were unable to pay and gave him mutton, sausage, squirrels, quail, and as noted in one story, one fat pig. The deep freeze stayed full all the time. And Doc really enjoyed all of the meat from the bartering as payment for his services. There were many patients over the years with as much doctoring out of the office as inside these offices. He was a familiar figure around town and at the hospital and stayed with his mission as long as he was able. When he was older, he went to his office half a day for several years and finally retired from part-time practice when he was almost 85 years old.

A medicine cabinet, a bed identical to those used in hospitals at the time, and sterilized instruments greeted patients who came in to see the nurse, who gave shots and medicine as prescribed by Dr. Cowart. A maroon leather couch and matching loveseat, along with several chairs, graced the waiting room. Also in this room, a bookcase housed medical texts and journals while pictures and plaques on the walls gave the patients something less cerebral to view as they waited.

Most of Doc's patients were referred to Rawls Drugstore for their prescriptions, just down the street from his office. Among the close circle of professionals that Doc also called friends were Inman Rawls, Sr. and Inman Rawls, Jr., owners of the drugstore. Miss Ina (Mrs. Rawls, Sr.) was especially thoughtful toward our family at Christmas, always delighting me with some unique gift.

Pink Powders

Perhaps more than any other medicine, the memory of the pink powders remains the most vivid to Doc's former patients. *Dorland's Illustrated Medical Dictionary* (25th ed.) defines a powder as "a substance made up of an aggregation of small particles, as that obtained by the grinding or trituration of a solid drug." We still have no idea what went into the pink powders. A childhood patient of Doc's, Shirley Holcomb Riley, remembers her mother putting the powders in a spoon and adding a little water. They tasted terrible, according to almost everyone who took them, but they worked.

Billie Hunter Smith, another childhood patient, remembers more than the powders in Doc's pharmaceutical fare for children:

> Before we started school in September, we had to take three pink powders. Caluma. And you couldn't have anything to eat after midnight and then you had to have the pink powders one hour apart and then the next hour you had to take Milk of Magnesia, black draught, or Epsom salts . . . He'd always say, "Clean out your stomach, and then we'll know where you are."

Buddy Moody was the apple of Doc's eye, an endearing great nephew he looked upon as he would his own son. Doc revealed a lot about the office life to him, such as the time he asked Doc about some little red pills that looked like red hots. Doc told him

DR. H. B. COWART
REGISTRY NO. 4709
OFFICE IN MASONIC TEMPLE   POPLARVILLE, MISSISSIPPI
PHONE: SW. 5.4791

FOR _____

ADDRESS _____ DATE _____

℞

HAVE THIS FILLED AT
RAWLS DRUG STORE   _____
M. D.

Doc's prescripton pad from his Poplarville office.

they were sugar pills that he gave to hypochondriacs and that they worked. Buddy felt special, being privy to this kind of information, and decided the sugar pills remedy was pretty smart.

One of Doc's most common remedies for sore throats was a cotton swab soaked in Mercurochrome. Family members were not excluded from this dreaded remedy; both Buddy and his sister, Miriam, remember this procedure. Miriam recalls:

> Bigum had a miniature mop that he dipped with Mercurochrome. You always gagged but it stopped the tonsillitis in its tracks. And remember, he wouldn't let us have our tonsils out because of the threat of polio. Frankly, I sometimes felt deprived, because other people were having theirs out and it seemed kind of a neat thing. Little did I know how smart, yet again, he was.

Almost as much as a shot, children dreaded this genuinely gagging experience, but like the powders, it worked. With Alexander Fleming's discovery of penicillin in 1928, the twentieth century already seemed light years ahead of the Victorian age, yet it would be another twenty years before antibiotics reached the masses. Childbirth and childhood disease, such as typhoid and scarlet fever, were the staples of a rural doctor's practice.

From Doc's first office in the room next to his father-in-law's store in Gwinville to his last, the suite in Poplarville, the era of modern medicine as he practiced it echoes a famous Rockwell painting in its simplicity. He had one of the earliest telephones in Poplarville, and his office number was 89. Miriam was impressed by a machine that was to the right of his desk, probably an early model x-ray machine. Doc's use of Dr. Titchenor's antiseptic in the office was legendary, as Mr. Martin Travis Smith, who was delivered by Doc in 1934, and who practiced law in Poplarville, remembers well:

> David Smith, my long-time law partner, practiced by himself and his office was with the City Hall, when it used to be in front of the Masonic temple. At coffee time I'd come in the back door of the Masonic temple and pass Doc's office . . . there was always that smell . . . just antiseptics . . .

And the medicine cabinet had no free samples from drug companies. Amazingly, several of the medicines people remember Doc prescribing for minor yet extremely annoying problems are still available at most drugstores. Icthamol, a thick, tar-like salve we used for skin irritations such as bee stings and burns, remains an inexpensive, effective treatment. Campho-Phenique was another favorite for dealing with insect bites. In response to a query placed in several newspapers in the fall of 2001, the following is a letter referring to one of Doc's more "natural" remedies:

Mosquito Bites

I was raised in the Fords Creek community, which is about 15 miles outside of Poplarville, Mississippi. Dr. Cowart was our family doctor; however, back then we didn't go to the doctor very much. My name is Ovetta Smith DeVries and I am 83 years old. I still own the old home place on Fords Creek. I go every spring and fall to visit and stay about two months at a time. My grandpa Jeptha was the one who built the house I still live in when I visit Mississippi. The house is now over 100 years old.

I was a WAC in the Army during World WarII stationed at Fort Benning, Georgia. I met my husband on a bus trip from Poplarville to Fort Benning. His name was Henry DeVries and he was also stationed at Fort Benning. Henry's first wife died before the war and they had two children. The two boys were living with their maternal grandparents in Poplarville while he was in the Army. We both got out of the Army about the same time and were married in Hattiesburg, Mississippi, on August 3, 1946. My husband's father who lived in Texas told him about jobs that were available in the refineries in Texas, so we traveled to Texas to see about getting a job. Once Henry had secured a job with the Texas Company (now Texaco), we went back to Mississippi to get the boys from their grandparents.

When we got the two boys, the baby boy, who was four at the time, had sores all over his body from mosquito bites and walking through the dew-covered grass early in the mornings. Before we started back to Texas, my husband carried him to Dr. Cowart in Poplarville. Dr. Cowart told him to put the boy in a bathtub filled with water and oatmeal. He said not to dry him off or rub off the oatmeal. He was to let the oatmeal dry on his skin. Within one week all the sores were gone.

Dr. Cowart in a Rockwell pose, Poplarville office (c. 1950s).

My request for Doc stories managed to reach Mrs. Mary Ann Herrington in New Albany, who read about it in *The Tupelo Journal*. Mary Ann's mother was Mary Nimocks Parker Bostwick, who was the daughter of Hubert and Callie (Batson) Parker; Mrs. Bostwick grew up in Poplarville. Mary Ann was visiting in Poplarville in the 1940s and Doc had to put stitches over her left eye after she fell in a concrete flowerpot on her grandmother's front porch. Mary Ann's father, Dr. Robert H. Bostwick, Jr., was from Lyman, just outside of Gulfport, and she remembers his talking about Doc and thinks they may have worked together for a short time.

Miriam remembers what many of those who have written to me remember about his manner:

> The main thing, of course, was the bedside manner. Kathryn [Miriam's mother] had so many life-threatening episodes; he and his nurse, sometimes, would appear, and either deal with the problem here at home, or take her to the hospital. To a child, this was scary, but if I could see Bigum, he would inspire such confidence in me—and I could tell in my parents—that the fear was diminished. His portly frame added to the "presence" that he posed when he entered a room. Even though he showed the same persona at the office, it was more powerful out in the field; maybe this is true for me because he was often here at home when we needed him so badly. There is almost no way to compare a contemporary doctor's office manner with his home-visit manner because not too many make house calls.

Not all of Doc's patients lent themselves to that Rockwell image of the family doctor. Various elements about Doc's practice placed him in a unique light, including his Saturday-night clientele. He often went up to his office to wait for the cut and wounded men who came out of the "juke joints." They came to him from places across the tracks, like the Blue Goose and the Blackjack, with names like Sugar Cookie and Whiskey Britches. They sought Doc because they knew he would help them, even if they had no money. He was skilled with a needle. As a teenager in the late 1950s, Buddy accompanied him to the office many Saturday nights, when things were slow at the movie house.

I kind of held him in awe . . . because he was a doctor and he could do things that most everybody else couldn't do and so many people depended on him. I remember looking at him as a child and even on up later on, that sewing the people up—I was just amazed at what ease he would do that—

Ben "Buddy" Solomon Moody

Between the ages of eight and twelve, Buddy was in and out of Doc's office for the usual childhood illnesses and accidents. One year after he had sold Christmas cards as a fundraiser, he received a small hatchet for a prize. The first day he played with it and he sliced his leg across the shin. His sister, Miriam, took him to Doc. He said this was his first experience with a "deadening shot," which Doc administered before he started sewing him up. His most vivid memory (besides the shot) was the ashtray in Doc's office made from a cow horn, no doubt a handmade gift from a patient. Frequent visits to our home made a similar impression on Buddy, which he says "was kind of a magic place."

J. M. Howard, Jr., remembers Doc's physicals for the high school boys who were trying out for football. At the time "Junior" went to the office for his physical, Doc was approaching eighty. "I walked in there and said, 'Dr. Cowart, I'm here to get my physical for football,' and he said, 'Well,' as he reached up and grabbed me by the shoulder, 'You had any broken bones lately?' I said, 'No sir.' He said, 'You been sick?' I said, 'No sir.' He said, "Well, I delivered you. There ain't nothin' wrong with you—go on and play football.'"

As a child, Junior helped Doc corral a patient. "I went with Tim Sanford to the doctor's one time and Tim had cut his foot . . . [Doc] was going to give Tim a shot—a tetanus—and Tim ran. Doc said, 'I'm too old to catch that boy; you go get him.' I caught Tim and brought him back."

The Bullet-Wound Walk-in

Junior's father, who had a butcher's shop on Main St., helped bring one of Doc's first patients into the office. Junior remembers hearing his father talk about an incident that he believes occurred in the thirties.

> He just happened to be walking by there and saw them unloading this guy . . . a man had been shot in the stomach with a rifle. Doc had just got there. They got him in the office and put him on the table . . . He said Doc put a hole big enough to fit a cannonball in and never did find the bullet. He said no organs were damaged and sewed him back up. When they started to lift him off the table onto a stretcher, Doc said, "Wait a minute," and told them to turn him over. There was a little lump in his back; Doc just pricked the skin and pulled the bullet out. The guy did fine.

Doc did not shy away from sending patients on for more specialized care and often diagnosed problems intuitively. This was the result of having extremely limited facilities when it came to tests. Fortunately, Doc was gifted in applying his training and seeing that people found the right kind of help. What he didn't have in facilities, he made up for by studying his patients' habits and being familiar with their family history. Billie Hunter Smith, the wife of a patient who benefited from his gift on a particular occasion, has never forgotten the day that Doc diagnosed her husband's ulcer and sent him on to Hattiesburg. Her husband, Hack, went straight from an important board meeting to Doc's office, with abdominal pain and nausea. Doc called the hospital in Hattiesburg to tell them he was sending a patient who would need to be seen immediately because of a bleeding duodenal ulcer. Mrs. Smith accompanied her husband to Hattiesburg and met the attending physician at the hospital.

> When I got there with him, he [the doctor] said, "Where are the x-rays?" I said, "We have no x-rays." He looked at me like I was crazy and lost my mind. He asked the second time . . .J. S. Moody came up there and he asked him. "Oh, he just looks at us and tells us what's wrong."

Once the hospital ran its tests and their results confirmed Doc's diagnosis, the attending physician told the Smiths he wanted to personally meet the doctor who so accurately diag-

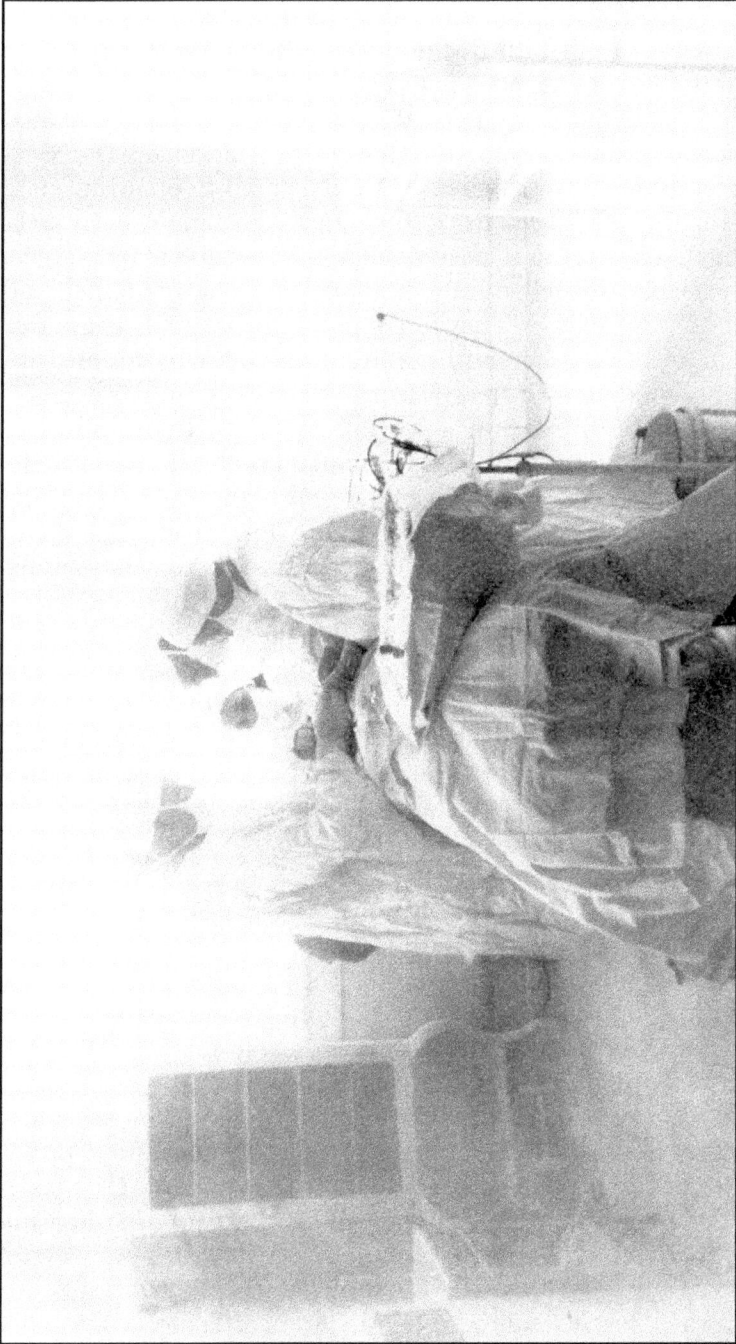

Dr. H. B. Cowart assisting Dr. Davis in surgery in the operating room at the Poplarville hospital (c. 1940).

nosed Mr. Smith's problem. At a later date, Doc drove to Hattiesburg to visit with this physician and received a personal tour of the hospital.

In June of 2002, Mr. Leonard Stanford of Poplarville related his family's connection to Doc that further illustrates Doc's extraordinary ties to his patients. Doc delivered Leonard in 1938 and over the years kept in close contact with family, even nicknaming Leonard "Bud." When Leonard was about four and a half years old, he fell from a tractor driven by his father and uncle and was run over. They took him to the hospital, where Doc saw him and called Leonard's father aside, advising him to take the boy immediately to New Orleans because his injuries were extensive and life-threatening. After taking him to Touro Infirmary in New Orleans by way of an ambulance also known as the Jenkins hearse, they waited five days and nights before knowing if he would make it. During that time, Doc traveled back and forth between Poplarville and New Orleans to better prepare for his return and treatment in Poplarville. Leonard eventually recovered, thanks to good care. In later life, he went to see Doc with a bad back. He said Doc told him he had a kidney stone and needed to go back to New Orleans. Doc gave him a shot for pain before Leonard started out and he passed the stone on the way to New Orleans. Leonard reiterated how Doc stood by him over the years and how much his family thought of Doc.

A Nurse's Sense of Humor

During his peak years in the Poplarville office, Doc was blessed with not only competent, but intuitive nurses at his side, who knew when to take the initiative. While many professions demand competency in initiative in those who hold a "right-hand man" position, few depend on that person to be as highly-trained as a nurse. Working side-by-side, as nurses and physicians tended to do during the years that Doc practiced, placed a great deal of strain at times on the nurse, particularly when the doctor had more than one emergency to handle. Ms. Myrna (Buddy) Paul was Doc's first nurse in Poplarville, starting with him in the Thirties, followed by Ms. Frances Poole. Ms. Lucille

Doc in his Poplarville office, 1960.

L-R: Nurse Myrna Paul, author Jane, and Doc on front steps of Masonic Temple, Poplarville (c. 1940).

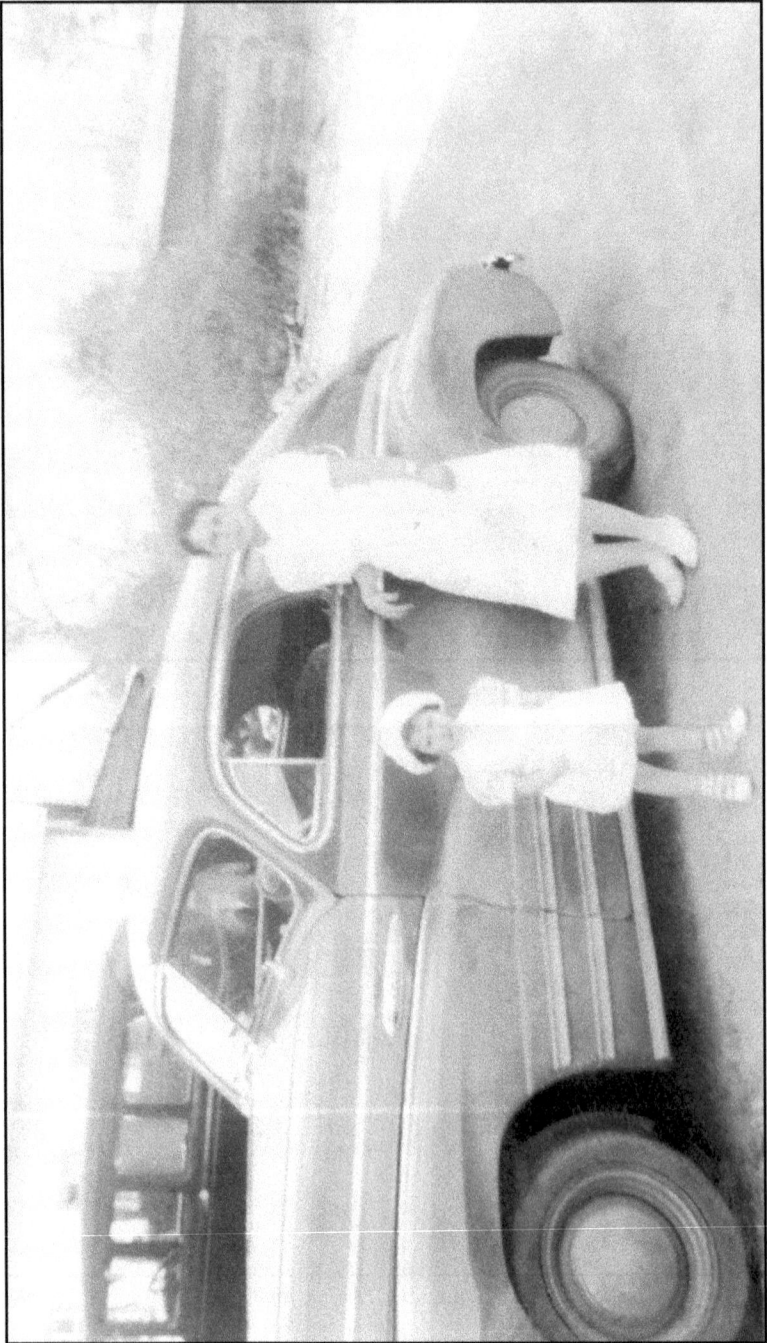

Author with Nurse Myrna Paul next to one of Doc's cars, 1940.

Doc standing in front of the Pearl River County Health Department (c. 1945).

Howard worked for Doc during the decades of the Fifties and Sixties. On several occasions, Ms. Lois Nobles, who worked for Dr. Davis at the hospital, accompanied Doc on emergencies. Between 1955 and 1960, Ms. Betty Alexander handled the office for Doc.

Dr. Cowart's best nurses shared a trait that helped them through times of great stress and endeared them to him: a sense of humor. Nurse Betty Alexander, who came to know Doc at the time when he was phasing out his house calls and seeing almost all patients at the office, remembers a wryness about him in the later years:

> One day I was going out at lunch and I got out there and I had two flats. I went back in and said something to him, that I had to make a phone call, that I had two flat tires, and he said, "Well, I don't know what it would be like to not have any luck. I guess it's better to have bad luck than none."

Just before this book went to press, I had a delightful conversation with Elizabeth Buckalieu Randle in Katy, Texas. She told me a very gratifying story about Doc going by bus to the Children's Home in Jackson, Mississippi, in 1933 to pick up Canadian twins her parents were to adopt. When he arrived, the twins were already taken so he picked out Elizabeth and carried her back on the bus to Poplarville to her proud parents. The wonderful ripple effect goes on.

In almost every small town in the South there are characters who span the generations and seem to have always been around. Such a person was Tap Bolton, who happily took on the role of helping anywhere he was needed in Poplarville. Now retired but still very much out and about, Tap was a tremendous help to Doc when driver Sim Poole was not there. Whether acting as a liaison within his neighborhood, church or at public gatherings, he had a take-charge attitude that came across as comedic. This was one of the reasons he got along so well with Doc. Today, Tap's colorful embellishing of the way things used to be remains one of his endearing traits to the people of Poplarville.

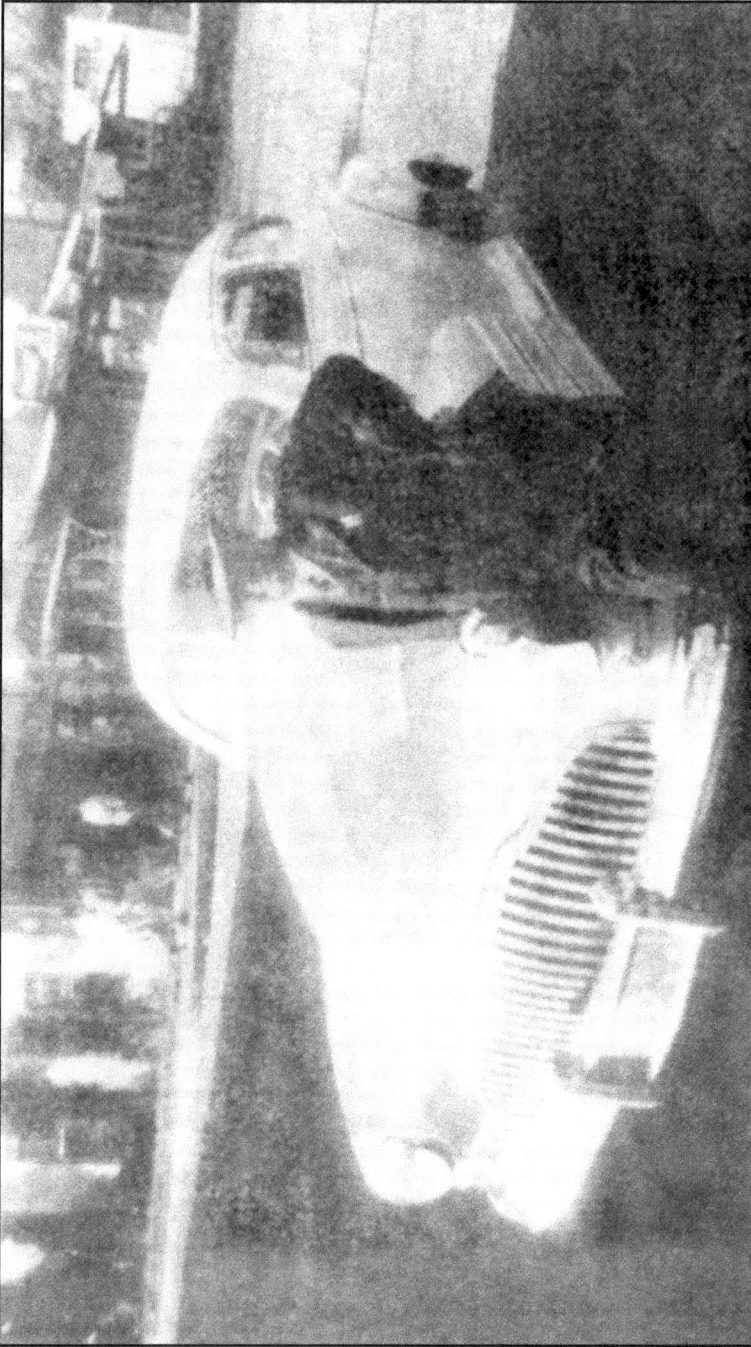

Doc standing in front of one of his Buicks. Many house calls were made in this car (c. 1950).

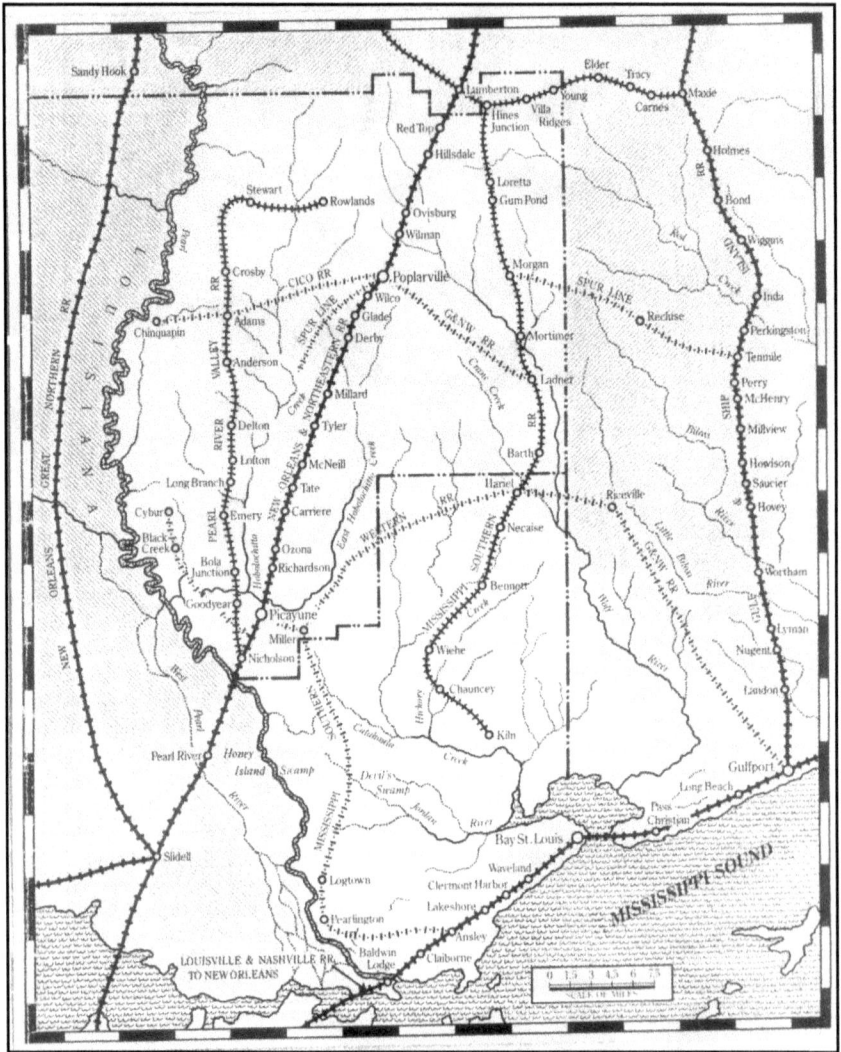

A map from the early 1900s, showing railroad and river communities in south Mississippi. Many of those Doc visited regularly are no longer on the map.

Chapter V

House Calls and Phone Calls

The lots may be cast into the lap,
but the issue depends wholly on the Lord.

Proverbs 16:33

In the 1970s my cousin Miriam experienced a rarity in any part of the United States, but particularly so for the heart of New York City. Their pediatrician made a house call to their residence on West End Avenue, in response to an emergency regarding their son. Their fears were quickly relieved by the presence of this trusted family friend, who diagnosed and treated their son on the spot.

In small pockets of the country, some physicians still make house calls, usually for elderly clients whose physical limitations restrict travel but who wish to live out their days in their residence rather than in retirement communities or nursing homes. Conversely, physicians who make house calls today in cities like Los Angeles and New York are more likely responding to patients of celebrity status or people who wish to protect their privacy and who can pay handsomely for the call.

On the one hand, the mobility of middle-class Americans, and even those living at the poverty level, has been a boon to the physician in private practice, eliminating the time and effort associated with house calls. On the other hand, the human element—getting to know the patient beyond the 15-minute office visit—has suffered, with the house call being replaced by the assembly-line atmosphere of most doctor's offices. Little did I understand how much the doctor on a house call imparted to his patient until I started getting letters from people who experienced that special treatment from Dr. Cowart. In response to an invitation I had printed in several newspapers in southern Mississippi last fall, letters about Doc came from the former patients as well as their descendents, from places like Nederland, Texas and New Albany, Mississippi. The first letter I received came from one of Doc's patients during the early years of his practice in Poplarville, Susie Parris Stringfellow. Susie married T. G. (Andy) Stringfellow in 1939 and in 1940, gave birth to her first child, a daughter, with the help of Doc and his nurse at the time, Ms. Myrna "Buddy" Paul. The delivery took place at the Stringfellow home, and the fee was $25.00. Like many of their neighbors during the Depression years, the Stringfellows were short on cash and had only $15.00 to pay Doc, with a promise to pay the balance in two weeks. Doc was unconcerned about the balance, so much so that when Mr. Stringfellow stopped by to make good on the promise, Doc said, "What did I do for you?" as if he'd forgotten about any debt.

Mrs. Stringfellow wrote that she had two more children delivered at home by Doc, and the charge was always $25.00, which she said they often laugh about: "If everyone had paid Doc what they owed him, he would have died a rich man." The Stringfellows still reside in Poplarville and both remember Doc's house calls as times they would never forget.

With surprise at the number of responses and gratitude to those who took the time to write about their memories of Doc, I opened several letters over the next few months.

Dear Jane,

I am 91 years old and moved to Poplarville when I married Norman Caver Rouse in 1934. Dr. Cowart was the H. K. Rouse's family doctor and he became ours as well. He delivered our babies at home and doctored their childhood diseases. After one delivery, I remember he stayed up real late one night with my husband to be sure all was well with both the baby and me.

The 30s were the depression years, and I doubt Dr. Cowart sent bills. Some people paid as best they could, with produce, some money or not at all.

Norman and Dr. Cowart were always good friends and he enjoyed going by and visiting with him when he paid what he owed the good doctor.

I knew your family well and they were held in high regard by the whole community. Your grandfather was not only a good doctor, but also an outstanding humanitarian. I'm so glad you are writing this tribute to him.

Sincerely,
Jeanette L. Rouse

Another patient from his early practice in Poplarville expressed a similar "debt of gratitude."

Allow me to introduce myself—my name is Mrs. Lloyd Walley and I live approximately seventeen miles from Poplarville. I am almost eighty-six years of age so God has blessed me.

I began using Dr. Cowart in the early 1940's. In February of 1945, Dr. Cowart delivered my first child, a daughter, who was born at the hospital in Poplarville. Due to my husband being in Uncle Sam's army it only cost me four dollars ($4.00), which covered the cost of my food, to have my daughter delivered.

In March of 1948 when time came for my second child (a son) to be born, I had requested Dr. Cowart come to our home to deliver this child. So Dr. Cowart and Nurse Lois Nobles drove the seventeen miles into the country and spent many hours with me before our son was delivered. I reached under my pillow and gave Dr. Cowart the twenty-five dollars ($25.00) that he charged for the delivery.

I developed some health problems and was told not to have any more children, but in May of 1952 with Dr. Cowart's help, I gave birth to our third child (a son). This son was born at the hospital for fear of my health problems. I felt a very strong debt of gratitude to Dr. Cowart for without his help and the good Lord's help I don't think I would be been able to give birth to this son.

There was a Dr. Cowart Day held in Poplarville, which honored him and all the children he had delivered during his medical practice. I can remember hundreds of people being there and marching in the parade down the streets of Poplarville.

I can also remember going to his house one Sunday so he could treat one of my sick... There aren't any doctors today that would measure up to Dr. Cowart and personal attention he gave his patient.

Hard times and the lack of cash among many of the families Doc tended gave a broader perspective to the phrase "debt of gratitude," when it came to Doc taking payment for his services. Nurse Betty Alexander remembers, "You know, I wonder how in the world he lived; I don't think anyone ever paid him . . . I really believe that a doctor probably makes more in a half a day now than he made in a month."

Steep Hollow and Other Stories

As Doc's fan mail grew during the fall of 2001, a letter from another 91-year old, Mr. Biser Smith, illustrated Doc's accessibility to his patients:

He took care of my whole family, even my Mom and Dad, William and Osula Smith with thirteen children. People of the community would always come and get me to call Dr. Cowart to come and take care of the problem.

Ben and Ada Smith of this community had gone to New Orleans to a doctor there for Miss Ada but they did not do anything for her. Mr. Ben asked me to come see him and he asked me if I would go get Dr. Cowart. He believed he could do her some good and I know if you ask him to come he will. I went to town to Dr. Cowart's house knocked on the door but did not get an answer. I then went into town and asked where he was and they said 'at home'. So I went back to his home and walked around to the back of the house and he and his wife were eating 'flap jacks'. He asked me to eat but I told him I would wait and drive him down since he was quite elderly at the time. He said, No, that's a nice drive down there and I'll bring my wife along so we can enjoy it together.

He took care of all the people in the Steep Hollow Community. Best of all, he was my buddy. If I ever needed anything or any type of counseling, I would go to him for his wisdom. He cared about people. I loved him.

From Asthma to Childbirth

Mr. Ralph Strahan remembers when his mother suffered from asthma and emphysema. He said Doc would come over at all hours to try and relieve her misery.

> Doc would jump out of bed and come in his pajamas and stay 'til she got relief, often one or two hours. This happened many, many times over the years—two to four a.m. We didn't have any money but it didn't deter him. He seemed to feel responsible for the community. Once I had a blocked sinus and I drove from New Orleans because I knew he would know what to do and soon. He gave me some pink medicine drops and shortly I was relieved. He was kind to everyone—just one big happy family.

In 1950, the year Doc was honored by the people of Pearl River County for nearly half a century of tending people in communities like Steep Hollow, Doc made house calls to a terminally ill man whose family still remembers those visits fifty years later:

> Doc was a good doctor and good to the people he treated. My Dad, Mr. G. H. Seal, was down six weeks before his death in March, 1950. We will always remember Doc coming in to treat him. He came fourteen miles in the country on a dirt road every night to check my Dad and drain his bladder. After treating my Dad, he would visit awhile and drink coffee and chew tobacco.
> We also used him with our babies. We carried our oldest child every day for a week at the time. Often times he didn't even charge for his visits.
>
> Margie and Earl Seal

> P.S.—When he came to check my Dad, he wouldn't even charge for the visit.

In the fall of 2001, I had the good fortune to interview Mrs.

Rose Gandy Lightsey, who was our back-door neighbor in Poplarville. She lived with her parents, Mr. and Mrs. A. M. Gandy, while her husband was overseas. Rose reminisced fondly about the unusual events that occurred with her children while her husband was away during the war. Doc had delivered her daughter, Linda, and her son, Butch.

The Coat Hanger and the Safety Pin

Rose laughed as she shared the stories of her calls to Doc about her children. When barely a toddler, Butch had put a wire coat hanger in his mouth. His cousin had jerked it out just as Rose entered the room. As he was bleeding at the mouth, Rose immediately ran to the phone to call Doc. Distraught, her first words came out, "Dr. Cowart, Butch swallowed a coat hanger!" Doc replied calmly, "Well, Rose, what was on it?"

A more serious incident within this same time period occurred with Linda, prompting a traumatic watch over a period of three days. After coming home from kindergarten one day, Linda crawled up on a bed next to her grandfather. She was dressing her doll and tried to close a safety pin with her teeth. Rose and the grandmother were in the kitchen cleaning up, when Linda apparently swallowed the safety pin. Much commotion followed, and Linda was rushed to Doc's office for an x-ray to determine if the pin was open or closed. The x-ray had to be taken to the hospital to be read; they were unable to locate the pin by the x-ray. Doc advised Rose and her parents to watch Linda closely and especially scrutinize her bowel movements. On the third day, the pin appeared in her stool and Linda seemed to suffer no ill effects from the open safety pin passing through her body.

During our interview, Rose commented "He was so good to me," talking about Doc's care for her and her family. Though I have heard many of his patients say this, he did seem especially protective of Rose as a patient. When she was five and a half months pregnant with Linda, she had to have an appendectomy, which was life threatening to her and the baby. Dr. Stewart performed the surgery with Doc present and Doc made the comment, "We can get another baby, but we can't get another Rose." Rose's sense of humor impressed both doctors after the surgery, when she demanded to know whether she was going to have a boy or a girl. In those days, the tests had not been developed to determine the sex of the unborn child and Rose's doctors nearly fell over when she put the question to them.

When he wasn't making house calls or seeing patients in the office, Doc was dispensing advice over the phone. Billie Hunter Smith recounts the time her son, H.A., was playing in a wading pool and stepped out of it into a fire ant bed. After being stung many times, he broke out into a rash from the bottom of his feet to his knees. Billie called Doc to ask what to do. He said, "Don't worry. Give him a good bath and put Campho-Phenique on the bites." Billie said she followed Doc's instructions and H.A. never had a blister. She remembers a similar piece of good advice from Doc when she called him about calming H.A while he was cutting teeth. Doc told her to give him a tablespoon of Milk of Magnesia. Again, she never had problems with him cutting teeth after this. Her trust in Doc was absolute. When it came time for H.A. to have a smallpox vaccination, Dr. Temple, the pediatrician in Hattiesburg, asked Billie if H.A. had had all of his shots. When she told him all but smallpox, he asked why not? She explained that Doc told her not to get that one for H.A. Dr. Temple agreed, that if Dr. Cowart said he shouldn't have it, he would not give it either. A school year went by and the second year, the Health Department said he was required to have the vaccination to attend school. The boy was given the vaccination and had a terrible reaction, contracting smallpox from the vaccination. He missed several days of school. Billie said they wondered how Doc knew that he would have that kind of reaction when the hospital told them that the chances of such a reaction were 10,000 to one. The answer was that Doc got to know his patients thoroughly and H.A. was one of many who benefited from this kind of care.

At a time when so many women gave birth at home and had little in the way of prenatal care before they delivered, Barbara Amacker Highstreet's mother was one of Doc's patients. Barbara remembers well the drama of her birth, as told to her by her mother, Mrs. Madie R. Gibson. Mrs. Gibson became ill on

Saturday and Doc told her to take a urine specimen to the nurse at the Health Department. This was done and the nurse confirmed it as being okay. Early Monday morning, Mrs. Gibson awakened with a backache. Thinking she was in labor, she sent her husband for the doctor. A neighbor came to stay with her in his absence. During this time she felt her face and mouth begin to draw to one side and the neighbor put a spoon in her mouth to supposedly prevent her from swallowing her tongue. When Mrs. Gibson began to convulse, however, the neighbor became frightened and ran home. Upon their arrival, Doc and his nurse, Myrna Paul, found Mrs. Gibson unconscious. After sending Mr. Gibson for more help, Doc delivered Barbara, and they took her mother to the hospital in a hearse, a vehicle that often served as an ambulance in small towns during this era.

Three days and eighteen convulsions later, Mrs. Gibson regained consciousness. Though Doc advised her against having more children, she gave birth to five more without incident. Decades later, Barbara consulted a medical text for an explanation of her mother's symptoms and determined that her mother had toxemia of pregnancy (eclampsia), a condition that produces convulsions that may involve twitching and produce a coma. She concluded that the wise doctor saved both her life and that of her mother.

Mr. Benjamin Slater recounted how a house call from Doc saved his life when he was two years old. He had ingested poison oak and his parents had "laid me out for dead . . . Doc stayed with me all night long and kept walking with me and brought me back to."

Like many people in positions of great responsibility, Doc's temper sometimes flared during high-stress situations. His nurses took the brunt of this, with good humor. Barbara recalls another story from her mother, who learned of another side to Doc's personality through Nurse Myrna Paul. Nurse Paul revealed an incident to her about accompanying the doctor on a house call to deliver a baby. When they arrived, several older women were sitting in the room with the patient. As the time neared for the baby's delivery, Doc had to get up on the bed to assist the mother. The bed fell down under their weight and Mrs. Paul laughed aloud. Doc looked at her and said, "You're fired!" According to Barbara's mother, she laughed in telling that he "hired me right back."

J. M. (Junior) Howard, Jr., who was a patient of Doc's from childhood through his early twenties, describes Nurse Lucille Howard as being another good-natured recipient of Doc's occasional eruptions. Doc and Nurse Howard were called to the home of a woman they knew to be carrying twins. Since the opportunity to deliver twins did not come along very often, Doc was anxious to be there for the birth. Shortly after their arrival at the house, where the patient was in labor, Doc was summoned to town to attend a victim of a terrible accident. According to Junior, "He told Miss Lucille, 'Don't you dare deliver those babies until I get back.' But he was gone longer than he wanted to be and Miss Lucille delivered those twins and it almost killed him."

Another story from Nurse Betty Alexander involves one of Doc's idiosyncrasies about driving: as he pulled into the spot outside his office after making a house call, he would never use his turn signal. Finally, she had to mention this observation to him one day. In a no-nonsense voice, he replied that "everyone knew" where he turned the car.

Car's in the Driveway, Baby's in the Bag

To say that cars were important to Doc is an understatement. I remember playing with the first electric window buttons on a Lincoln he owned. Whatever the latest gadget was, he had it. It seemed to me when he didn't wear out his cars on those country roads, he was trading for a new model every six months, and the tires stayed muddy a lot.

While most of Doc's patients who remember when he made house calls can describe which car he was driving, one of his first patients, Mr. Benjamin Slater, remembers what may have been Doc' s first car.

I don't know what year he bought his first car. First car I'd ever seen . . . had a chain drive like a bicycle, and there were solid tires—there was no air in them—and he had a little car horn on

Sim Poole, Doc's driver and friend, 1963.

the side of it that you'd blow by squeezing it with your hand . . .
That coupe he had, he'd go into a little stream of water and once
it drowned out and he got out and came to our house . . .
changed clothes and went to bed and went to sleep.

Mr. Slater later retrieved Doc's car, a Model T, from the
stream and brought it to their house.

Kathryn's description of her uncle's affiliation with cars is
quintessential:

Uncle Ben always drove a fine automobile; if you can think of the first cars as fine, and beyond to the time when he could afford the world's longest convertible. It was never long enough though to escape the tobacco juice that he spat at the intervals as he rode to a house call. There is a private joke that was often repeated about how Uncle Ben would walk out of his office, go to his car, back out without ever looking behind him. One of his neighbors in a store downtown used to park directly behind him until he discovered that was Uncle Ben's private parking lot. He simply got his car repaired several times without mentioning the problem to Doc.

Many of the people interviewed, as well as those who have written letters about Doc, state that he must have been one of the first people in southern Mississippi to own a car. Mr. E.R. Walker, writing for the *Simpson County News,* believed the first car he saw Doc drive—a Brush Sprocket, probably of 1910 vintage—was the first car many people in the county had ever seen. Martin Travis Smith, who rode in the back seat of Doc's car from time to time as a child, recalls the gunmetal-gray Lincoln-Zephyr that Doc owned. An impressive 2-door coupe, it was one of the many long, powerful cars that Doc preferred. This young passenger, who would later practice law in the building adjacent to Doc's office, recalls Doc's habit of chewing tobacco and spitting out the window, which left an indelible impression on the back-seat passengers. In the days before air-conditioning, all the windows in the car were rolled down in the warmer months and the tobacco juice often came back in on the passengers.

Doc was a good sport about most things, earning him a nickname from his good friend and chauffeur, Sim Poole. This kind, large black man came into my grandfather's life when he was beginning to slow down on the house calls. His most well-known phrase about Doc was "He's a spo't." Sim's hearty laugh could be heard often in our home, as he visited on a regular basis, sometimes staying for meals. He especially liked to draw Doc out on certain topics, as much to listen to the inflections in Doc's voice as his expressions. One such expression was the term "jack leg," which Doc used to describe ministers he didn't think were all they should be. Kathryn Moody remembers Sim: "Uncle

Doc's medical bag, which he was carrying when Sim Poole, Jr. was told by Poole, Sr. that the baby was in the bag.

Ben's driver was a dear friend whose name was Sim Poole. No road was too bad, nor was any place too remote for those two to maneuver. But, when it came to going to New Orleans (which they often did), they went in style."

Though Sim Poole was a much younger man than Doc, he died just a year before Doc, in 1969. In the fall of 2001, I had the chance to visit Sim Poole, Jr. in Poplarville. The first thing I saw was a big, maroon Buick Roadmaster in the driveway. Years ago, Sim Poole's son remembered Doc driving such a car and decided one day, he would have a car just like it. He also re-members being in awe of the size of the bag Doc carried on his rounds. He and a group of children were playing nearby when Doc went to a house to deliver a baby. Poole, Jr. asked his father why the doctor carried such a big bag. His father told him the baby was in the bag and Doc was taking it to the mother and father.

Chapter VI

Dr. Cowart Day

Never think you've seen the last of anything.
Eudora Welty, from "The Optimist's Daughter"

On May 6, 1950, approximately 6,000 people gathered in Poplarville, Mississippi to attend the Dr. Cowart Day celebration. According to a number of sources at the time, Dr. Cowart had delivered over 4,000 babies in his 45-year practice. Surrounded by a portion of the people he had helped bring into the world and seated next to his wife, Bertha, Dr. H. B. Cowart grinned from ear to ear as people came to show their gratitude and enjoy the activities associated with recognizing his service to them. Patients, friends and acquaintances of all ages and backgrounds were there to honor the doctor who not only delivered their babies, but who responded to their medical needs—whatever they were—at all hours.

Several newspapers carried coverage of this special day. Mr. Murphy Weir, editor of *The Poplarville Democrat,* which was known as *The Weekly Democrat* in 1950, gave the celebration headline status, with articles promoting the event and the dignitaries attending. Similar articles appeared in *The Commercial Appeal* of Memphis, *The Times-Picayune* of New Orleans, *The*

VOL. 17—NO. 35   THE WEEKLY DEMOCRAT, POPLARVILLE, MISSISSIPPI, THURSDAY, MA

DR. COWART DAY MEETING WITH WIDESPREAD APPROVAL OVER AREA

Served Almost Half A Century . . . .

Announcement of the program on Saturday, May 6, to honor Dr. H. B. Cowart has met with widespread approval as people from the entire area have offered assistance and expressed plans to attend during the day.

Likewise, the call for donations of meat animals and money with which to make the day a success is meeting with response. W. C. Stafford, general chairman of the event already has pledged a number of calves, hogs, and sheep, as well as money in hand, donated by people over the county.

Plans call for a parade for Dr. Cowart's "babies," speaking by Ed Patterson and John D. Smith, with Toxey Hall as master of ceremonies, and a barbecue with enough food to feed the throngs expected here. Music will be furnished by the college band. Signs will be posted along the streets,

banners over the highways leading to town and publicity in many papers are a part of the advertising program in connection with the day.

A number of quartets are being asked to come and help entertain the crowds during the day.

Tables and speaking stands are to be built on the grounds of the Community Center to accomodate the day's events.

All of the program will be based around genial Dr. Cowart and his 40 years of service to the ill of South Mississippi. Dr. Cowart is one of a vanishing clan of country doctors whose skill and understanding of humanity has administered to white and colored through all hours of the day and night. The entire day is to be spent in giving recognition to that service and expressing the gratitude of a people for the man.

DR. H. B. COWART

March, 1950 newspaper article about Dr. Cowart Day. The Weekly Democrat was only one of several newspapers that covered Dr. Cowart Day before and after the event of May 6, 1950.

Clarion Ledger of Jackson, and *The Hattiesburg American*. While most of those attending were well aware of Doc's reputation for getting to know his patients, the media coverage of Dr. Cowart Day emphasized his reach beyond Pearl River County, stating that he answered calls day and night in Marion, Jefferson Davis, Hancock, Stone, and Lamar counties as well. In the fall of 2001, Mrs. Reba Pritchett of Poplarville sent me several newspaper clippings she had saved from the event, along with the comment, "Doc delivered my two sons, James in 1946 and Jessie in 1949. We loved Dr. Cowart and his wife and daughter."

With the Pearl River College band in the lead, a parade started the celebration that morning at 10:30. About 1500 of the babies Doc had delivered, ranging in age from infants to 40-year olds, followed the parade down Main Street. Doc watched and waved from the front porch of the Masonic Temple, where he had maintained an office suite for 22 years in Poplarville. Still hearty at 65, Doc maintained a practice as much devoted to rural bedsides as receiving patients at clinics and hospitals. Of the thousands who jammed Poplarville for this celebration, many attended who had relied upon his counsel for personal problems as much as his medical expertise for physical problems.

As if led by a 20th-century pied piper, the parade-goers proceeded to the Jaycee picnic grounds, where six speeches and two tons of barbeque awaited them. Flanked by state highway patrol cars, the parade ended at the Community Center grounds, where Toxey Hall, Master of Ceremonies and an attorney from Columbia, Mississippi gave an opening address at 11:15. Mr. Hall described Dr. Cowart as "an outstanding doctor and an outstanding citizen of Mississippi."

Following Mr. Hall's speech, State Highway Commissioner John D. Smith lauded Doc's commitment to his patients over the years and spoke warmly of their long friendship. Ed Patterson, retired Monticello attorney and another life-long friend, spoke of Doc's character, relating much of the history of

The marching band and parade of babies honoring
Dr. Cowart's forty-four years of practice. May 6, 1950.

his boyhood. Leopold Locke, Poplarville attorney, presented a plaque commemorating Doc's lengthy service and spoke of the esteem people of this county had for Dr. Cowart.

Under the noonday sun, the throng feasted on mutton, beef, and pork generously donated by various individuals. While Pete Carver took charge of the cooking, home demonstration ladies under the direction of Miss Lanelle Gaddis served the

Dr. Cowart waves to his "babies" from the steps in front of the Masonic Temple, Dr. Cowart Day, May 6, 1950.

crowd. Behind the scenes, General Chairman of the Day W. C. Stafford contributed his organizational skills, insuring that the day would not only be a crowd-pleaser but a lasting memory among those who came. J. S. Moody also played a big part in preparing this special day for Doc.

Jim Stanford, (1908-1991), was recognized as the oldest boy baby Doc had delivered in Pearl River County. One of the letters I received from people who remember that day came from Mr. Stanford's daughter:

Dear Jane,
    A cousin saw your article in the Poplarville paper and sent it to me.
    My father, Emmitt Jennings (Jim) Stanford was the first baby Dr. Cowart delivered. He was the 10th child of Maggie Murphy and Tack Stanford. They lived between the Ford's Creek and the Springhill communities.
    Years later, Jim married Nadine Smith during the Depression. Dr. Cowart delivered all three of their children at home in the Ford's Creek community. They were Hazel, Jewell, and Mary Margaret. Dr. Cowart was paid with a fat pig for one of their deliveries because they didn't have any money.
    I remember the night that Mary Margaret was born. I was almost three years old. I woke up, stumbled into the bedroom where there was fire in the fireplace. Mother showed me the new baby that Dr. Cowart had brought. I started putting on my black patent leather shoes and white and green striped socks and announced that I was going to live with Dr. Cowart. Mom and Dad persuaded me to stay.

Sincerely,
Hazel Stanford Edwards

Ironically, another man who was in the crowd was actually delivered by Doc three years earlier than Mr. Stanford, but was unaware at the time he held that distinction. In November of 2001, I met and interviewed that man, Mr. Benjamin Slater of Gwinville, Mississippi. Mr. Slater attended local schools and married Joan Elizabeth Smith in 1925. While Mr. Slater worked in the lumber industry, he and his wife raised three daughters and a son. He retired from Plantation Pipe Line Company in 1962 and still resides where he grew up.

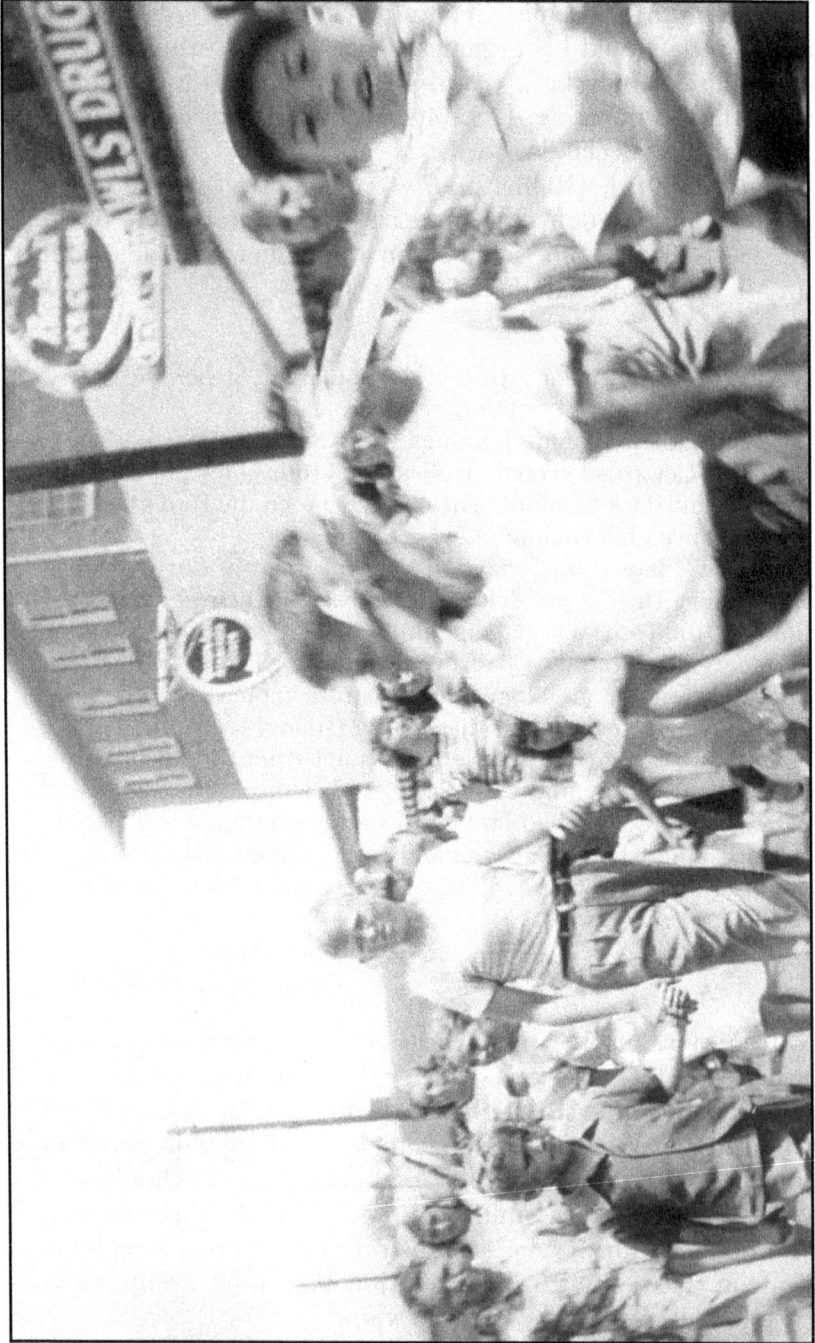

More parade-goers, Poplarville, Mississippi, May 6, 1950.

Garrett Snuff

Of the many speeches given that day, Mr. Slater remembers a particular anecdote told by Toxey Hall. The attorney was one of many of Doc's friends who seemed never at a loss when asked to speak about Doc. Mr. Hall had everyone's attention when he started to describe a method of delivering a baby, the Doc Cowart way. After arriving at the home of a patient in an advanced stage of labor, Doc would run a small amount of Garrett snuff under the mother's nose, causing her to sneeze hard. This method seemed to work well in aiding the mother when it came time to push the baby out of the womb. Though this powdered preparation of tobacco is more popular today among those who dip—that is, rub it on the teeth and gums—the practice of inhaling snuff was more popular among its earliest users, in seventeenth-century England. As its popularity became more widespread during the eighteenth century, its manufacture made a millionaire out of the descendents of John Garrett in the nineteenth and twentieth centuries, due to its popularity among tobacco users of the South. The Garrett snuff anecdote was only one of many characterizations of Dr. Cowart that came to me from people who attended the festivities that day.

Virginia "Ginger" Holston shared the following:

Dr. Cowart delivered me on October 17, 1941 at home. Sixteen months later he delivered my sister, Frances Greer (Hyde) on February 13, 1943. We lived at the Mississippi Experiment Station at White Sand (about 18 miles west of Poplarville). Most of the babies delivered during this time were in homes instead of hospitals . . . Dr. Cowart also delivered my husband, Curtis Holston, on February 18, 1939 and his sister, Theta Holston (Egnew) on August 10, 1943. They were all delivered at home. The Holstons lived about eight miles north of Poplarville in the Springhill community. Dr. Cowart made house calls in a wide radius from Poplarville. Babies were not often born at convenient times of circumstances. I am sure he traveled at odd times in difficult weather and transportation conditions and waited many long hours to deliver a baby. Even today, a home delivery would be difficult under the best conditions.

When I was about eight years old and Curtis was ten, there

Plaque presented to Doc on Dr. Cowart Day. Poplarville, Mississippi. May 6, 1950.

Dr. Cowart Day honorees: Mrs. J. H. O'Callahan and Mr. Jim Stanford, the two oldest babies delivered by Dr. Cowart in Pearl River County (May 6, 1950).

was a Dr. Cowart Day in Poplarville. We were in the parade but did not know each other then. He [Curtis] rode his bicycle and I walked. We laughed later when we discovered that the same doctor had delivered us at our homes and we participated in the same event to honor Dr. Cowart.

A favorite family story concerns Curtis's father and Dr. Cowart. Big Curt had a toothache and went to Dr. Cowart to have it pulled. Dr. Cowart tried to persuade Curt to go to the dentist, Dr. Arledge, to have it pulled, but Curt insisted that Dr. Cowart pull the aching tooth. Nurse Lucille Howard often laughed about this incident, a witness to Dr. Cowart putting pliers (or some sort of grippers) on Curt's tooth. Curt was very tall and lanky (6'7"). Every time Dr. Cowart would try to pull the tooth, Curt would come out of the chair. He followed Dr. Cowart all around the room for twenty to thirty minutes before the tooth was successfully extracted. At a time when specialists did not come to the more rural parts of the country, Dr. Cowart performed the duties of a general practitioner, surgeon, dentist, obstetrician, gynecologist, and pediatrician.

In addition to marching in the parade, children like Virginia and Curtis had a wealth of activities to enjoy that afternoon. The Poplarville pee-wee baseball team and Legion junior team defeated teams from Picayune at the Community Center grounds. An aerial show as well as a band concert entertained the celebrants. The festivities climaxed with a square dance, staged on the tennis court that evening.

And so the celebration all added up to a big day during which neighbors who had not seen each other for years came together for a host of traditional southern activities. Within the week, *The Weekly Democrat* published a thank you letter from Doc:

> I can never find words to really express my sincere appreciation to all you fine people for the way you honored me last Saturday in The Dr. Cowart Day. I can never be completely worthy of all that you have done for me and it makes me want to work even harder to live up to the things you did for me. I am truly grateful and it shall always be a warm spot in my heart.

Mr. Benjamin Slater, at ninety-six years, the oldest living baby delivered by Dr. H. B. Cowart, and his daughter, Bonnie Slater Miller. November, 2001.

I cannot close without giving credit to whatever success I have achieved and service that I may have rendered, to the fine nurses who have accompanied and assisted me in treating you. They deserved gratitude for their unselfish efforts and have contributed much.

Dr. H. B. Cowart

To sum up the man honored on Dr. Cowart Day: he was of an era of medicine that is obsolete. He knew his patients, their lifestyles, emotional makeup, beliefs, and even their dietary habits. This daily knowledge of people accounted somewhat for an uncanny ability to diagnose their problems with little or no help from modern technology. He always saw people from the big-picture perspective, or in the words of Junior Howard, "He doctored the whole person, not just the body."

Passing the Torch

Of those who remember Doc from his later years, the comparison to the Norman Rockwell painting of the family doctor comes from more than one source. Dr. Willie Stringer, a physician who came to Poplarville on the heels of Doc's last years of practice, made such reference about Doc's physical impression on people during an interview in the fall of 2001. Dr. Stringer set up practice in Poplarville in 1957, hoping to build his clientele on the recommendations of Dr. Cowart. With the exception of making house calls and delivering babies, Doc was still practicing full time at the age of seventy-six. In Dr. Stringer's estimation, the number of babies Doc had delivered by the end of the 1950s had climbed to 5,000, and this was a conservative estimate.

Dr. Stringer expressed sincere gratitude for Doc's help with starting his own practice and talked with regret that he felt that his practice could not allow him to keep the kind of schedule Doc did with house calls. Doc's devotion to weekly visits with Ran Batson, as well as a few other people in the community, moved Dr. Stringer. Doc was a "refined person," in Dr. Stringer's words, when it came to socializing and getting to know his patients. Comparing himself to Doc, he said, "I'm a country dude."

Dr. Stringer summed up Dr. Cowart thus: "One thing that probably contributed to that [Doc's ability to relate to his patients, no matter what their station in life] . . . was that all he ever wanted to do was see patients."

Doc greets the people who came out to see him on Dr. Cowart Day.

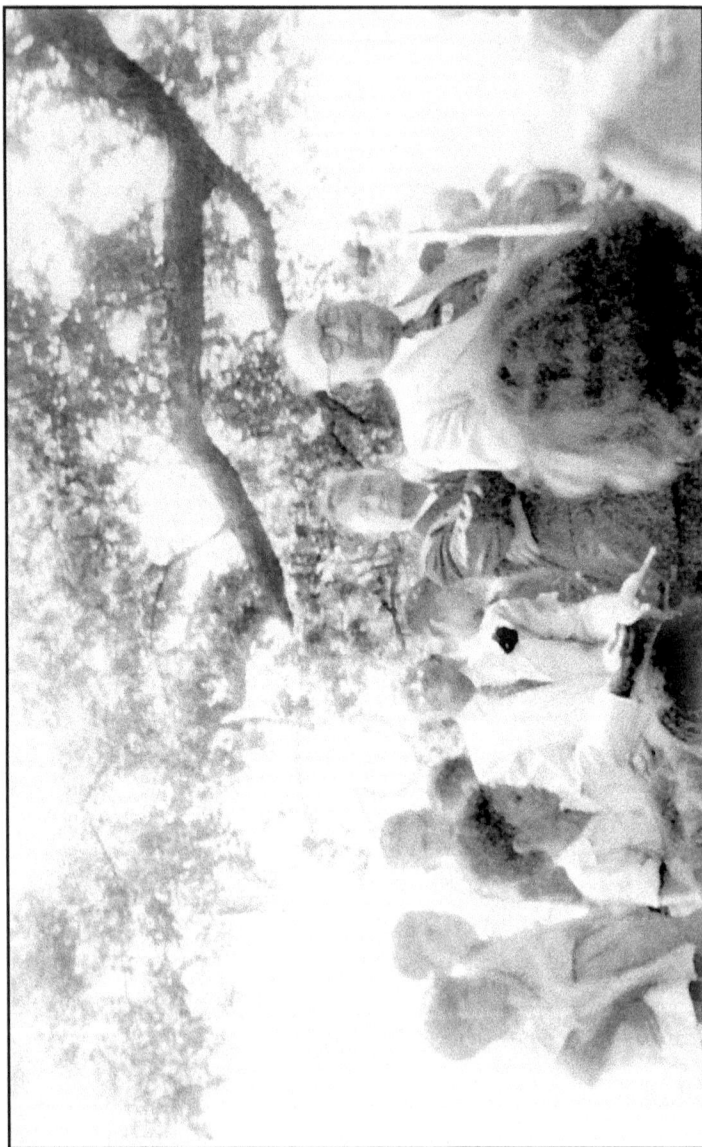

Speech-making at the community center, Poplarville. May 6, 1950.

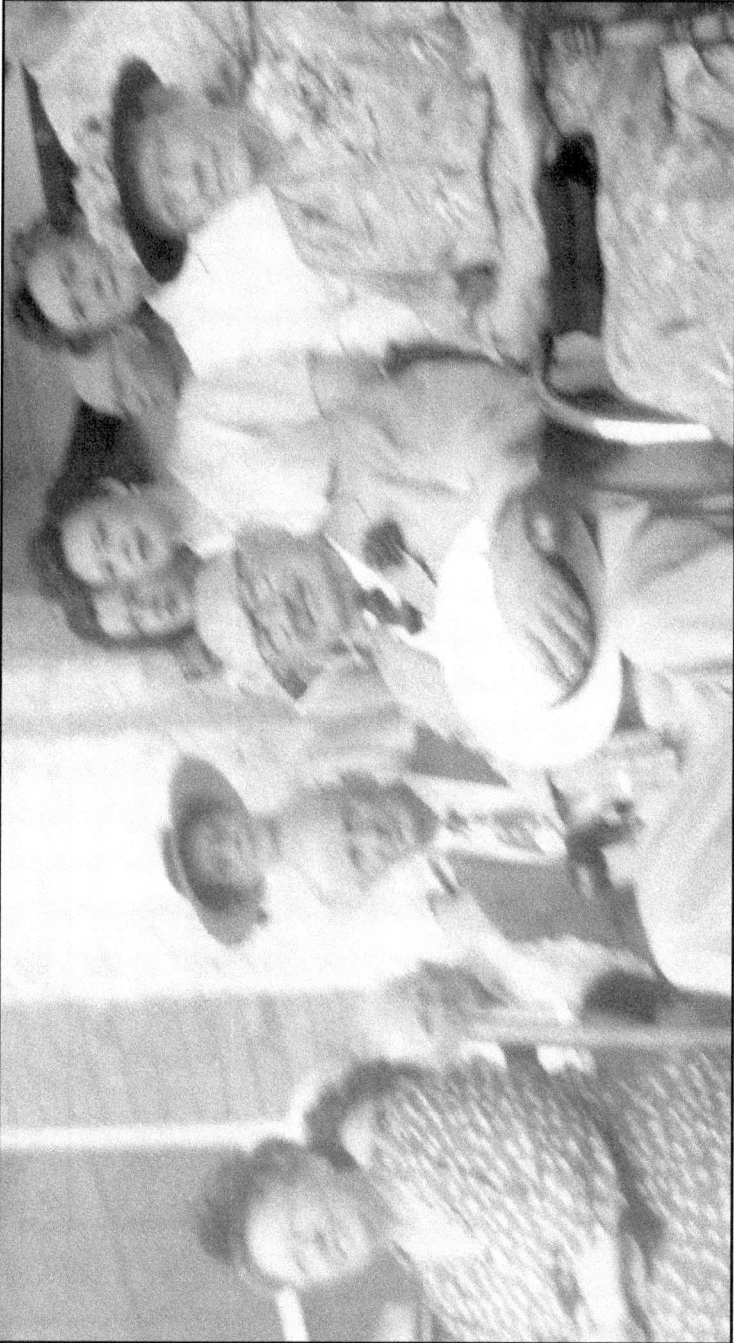

(Front center and right) Doc and Maudie seated on the porch in front of the Masonic Temple, watching parade pass for Dr. Cowart Day.

Doc and Maudie viewing the parade for Dr. Cowart Day, May 6, 1950.

Chapter VII

Politician

There is a mysterious cycle in human events. To some generations much is given. Of other generations much is expected. This generation has a rendezvous with destiny.

Franklin D. Roosevelt
Presidential Nomination Acceptance Speech
June 26, 1936

Between World War I and World War II, the strongest nation in the world experienced a major setback both financially and psychologically. For all its wealth and high standards of living, America had to take a step back during the years of the Depression, opening a new era for the power of politics to flourish.

Doc was neither a yellow-dog Democrat nor a Scalawag Republican, as his father had once been labeled, but he understood and enjoyed the machinations of politics. Part of his routine involved studying political issues in the Jackson *Clarion Ledger* before leaving the house every morning. Though he never ran for political office, he stayed abreast of issues and leaders to the extent that he was looked upon as an influential member of the community, particularly when it came to support at rallies. He sought politicians' company when the issue was one that affected his community, and, while it would have been easy for him to be a "yes" man to a particular party or candidate, he chose to delineate between the issue and the personality. His strategy involved going as far as he could to the highest political authority, absorbing all he could about government plans for improving a situation, and bringing it to a local level of awareness. Franklin D. Roosevelt's New Deal programs were of special interest to him and the citizens of southern Mississippi.

Of the programs established during the Depression years, Doc believed that one of the best was the CCC (Civilian Conservation Corps). He saw the strength of such a program from the beginning, not only because it would benefit a part of the country whose economy was so dependent on the timber industry but also because it would employ a segment of the population in desperate need of jobs. Under the Army's control, the CCC commanders were addressed as "Sir" by corpsmen and had disciplinary powers. Ironically, this paramilitary discipline would serve the corpsmen well when so many were called to serve in World War II. With more than 500,000 young men living in these camps by 1935, most staying from six months to a year, the impact was felt in Mississippi as well as the rest of the country. Doc's faith in this "tree army," whose efforts varied from planting trees to building canals and ditches as well as wildlife shelters, appears to have been justified, in view of the current economic base supporting forest recreation and industry in south Mississippi.

Doc's confidence in and promotion of programs created during Roosevelt's presidency extended to The Works Progress Administration as well as the WPA Youth Administration. The seven-year history of this program yielded jobs for millions and, though the jobs were temporary and Pearl River County participants represented a small percentage when compared to the rest of the nation, its implementation contributed to significant improvements in the community. Although established under the Emergency Relief Appropriation Act of April 1935 to create public jobs for the unemployed, responsibility for the unemployable, such as children, the aged, and the disabled, was returned to the states. With the emphasis on projects that could be accomplished without competing with private business, the WPA concentrated on building streets, highways, bridges, and public buildings, as well as restoring forests and extending electrical power to rural areas. The WPA National Youth Administration (NYA) gave work to nearly a million students; the Federal Theatre, Arts, Music, and Writers' Projects brought music and drama to the smallest communities, commissioned public sculptures, paintings, and murals, sponsored surveys of national archives, and produced a series of state and regional travel guides.

The scope of the WPA was unprecedented, its popularity a contributing factor to Franklin D. Roosevelt's resounding electoral victory in 1936. With growing prosperity in the 1940's, the WPA became increasingly difficult to defend, leading to its termination in 1943.

One of Doc's proudest moments of political involvement came from his association with the BAWI (Balance Agriculture with Industry), a prime example illustrating the issue being more compelling than the individual. Led by a retired lumberman, Hugh L. White, who later became Governor (1936-40; 1952-56), this plan for bringing industrialization to the rural counties of Mississippi was based on personal experience in his hometown of Columbia, Mississippi, where his business enterprises comprised a large portion of the economic base of the area. A recent article from Economic Development Review (Fall, 2000) sums up the effect of the BAWI program:

> [It] set the stage for the debate over state industrial incentives programs that emerged throughout the United States. Long before the Depression hit America in the 1930s, Mississippians had lived in a stagnant, arguably repressive economic environment. For the majority, life in Mississippi was one of rural poverty. In a way, the Mississippian's poverty was the poverty of the times . . . The social and economic programs unleashed in the wake of the Depression began to alter this situation, and of the many ways up and out of the economic quagmire, industrialization began to be viewed as the surest and quickest.

Doc served on the staff of Governor White as well as those

of Governors Thomas L. Bailey (1944-46) and Fielding L. Wright (1946-52). Such affiliation afforded him insight and opportunity when it came to promoting issues he felt would benefit the people of Pearl River County and surrounding communities.

Doc's interest in government-sponsored programs extended to Operation Bootstrap, a federally funded effort initiated after World War II. This program offered veterans and their families access to a free college education and low-cost access to housing on campuses. Doc was quite instrumental in getting that program to Pearl River Community College where a "married dorm" still testifies to the comprehensive nature of that effort. As much as possible, he provided free medical care to those in the program. Instead of telling a lot of people who to vote for, he chose a wiser way, and with a little help from a few strategic people, he helped the good rise to the top.

Further information regarding this program came from Fran M. Sheridan, Lead Guidance Counselor at Robins Air Force Base, Georgia:

> The voluntary Education Bootstrap policy allowing Air Force members to attend institutions of higher learning in full-time status, originated in the late 1950s/early 1960s, to assist pilots (officers) in their pursuit of a bachelor/master's degree. It was later changed in the 1960s to include enlisted personnel that wished to complete courses and/or a bachelor's degree in order to apply for a commissioning program. In 1985, an Educational Leave of Absence (ELA) program was incorporated under U.S.C. Title 10 that was similar in many respects to the AF Bootstrap Program. Due to questions from Air Force members on the ELA program, a USAF/JAG reviewed the Educational Leave of Absence and Bootstrap policies and determined the current bootstrap policy could not continue without compliance with the educational leave policy.

Reflecting on the genuine pleasure we always derived from the political rallies, with the food, the crowd, and the speakers, I am convinced that someone had to stir the pot a long time ahead, and that someone in Poplarville was Doc.

Doc wearing cape designed for Colonels on Mississippi Governor's staff (c. 1940s).

Program cover from Governor's Inaugural Ceremonies, Jackson, Mississippi, 1952. Far left—Dr. H. B. Cowart; Far right—J. S. Moody.

Governor Hugh White's staff, Jackson, Mississippi, 1952. Doc can be seen in the lower left corner, with one of his canes.

Doc receiving Presidential citation for selective service from Lonnie Smith and military representative, 1968.

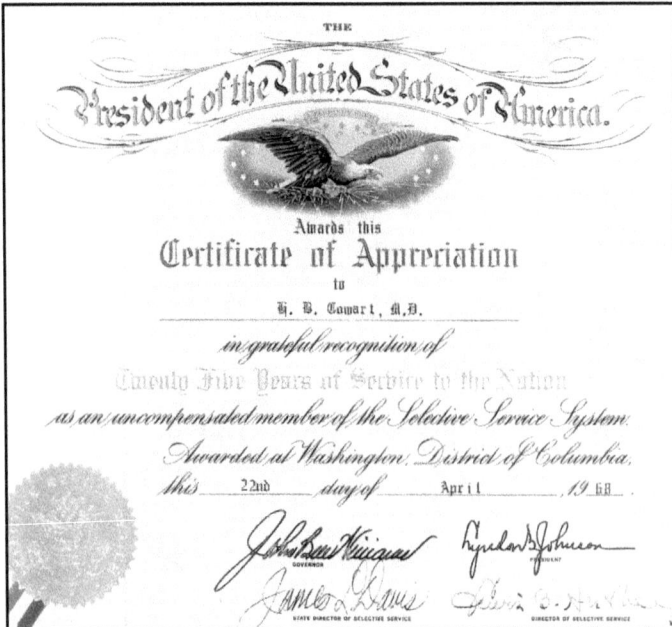

Presidential citation awarded Doc in 1968 for his twenty-five years of selective service.

Chapter VIII

A Historical Sketch of Poplarville, Pearl River County, and Pearl River Community College

A morsel of genuine history is a thing so rare as to be always valuable.
Thomas Jefferson, in a letter to John Adams (1817)

In 1965, as Doc's life and livelihood drew to a close in Pearl River County, a local writer published a tribute to the area titled *Next Door to Heaven*. To paraphrase S. J. Thigpen's book, there are some who think the good old days were when a mother would get up early, cook breakfast for a large family, fix lunches for several children, get them to school, milk the cows, clean up and never think for a minute that she was overworked. A farmer would turn his lawn over to the care of a good milk cow, the animal keeping it low and fertilized while giving quantities of rich milk and butter. A man was valued for his skill to chop wood, his marksmanship with a gun, the amount of cotton he could pick in a day, and the number of bushels of corn he could grow on an acre of land.

Every generation has its unique perspective on what was good and not so good about the past. For me, growing up in Poplarville in the shadow of my larger-than-life grandfather gave me a rose-tinted view of this community that only deepens with return visits to the area. In homage to Poplarville and Pearl

River County, I offer the following historical narrative that weaves the early history of this area with the first half of the twentieth century, when Dr. Cowart was a familiar traveler down long-forgotten roads.

Six Flags Over Hancock and Pearl River Counties

If you could have driven the present route of Highway 11 down through Mississippi in 1810 you would have passed out of the United States and into another nation when you drove through what is now Lumberton. As you drove on south through what is now Poplarville, McNeill, Carriere, Picayune, Nicholson, Pearl River, and Slidell you would have been traveling through West Florida until you reached the middle of Lake Pontchartrain, when you would have re-entered the territory of the United States.

The history of that part of South Mississippi lying south of the 31st degree of latitude is very different from the history of any other section of the United States. The old line of demarcation between the English possessions, and the French and then the Spanish, was the 31st degree of latitude, which is the present northern boundary of Pearl River County. By right of discovery, France had long laid claim to all this region but not until January 1699, was a move made to possess and occupy it. At that time D'Iberville anchored off of what is now the Mississippi Coast. He had been sent by the French government to explore and colonize Louisiana. He established his headquarters at Biloxi, which became the first capitol of Louisiana. The whole area remained under the dominion of France until on March 10, 1763, by the Treaty of Paris, France surrendered to England all her possessions in North America east of the Mississippi River. At the same time Spain surrendered to England her colonies of East and West Florida. Over the years, thousands of Americans had settled up and down both sides of Pearl River as well as the territory between the Pearl and the Mississippi under grants from both the Spanish and British governments. President Madison in October, 1810, no longer fearing the waning power of Spain, issued a proclamation declaring that West Florida was within the boundaries of Louisiana and directed Governor Claiborne of Orleans territory to take civil and military possession of the same. In pursuance of these orders Governor Claiborne took over West Florida without opposition. The American settlers had accomplished their main objective—the placing of their territory under the jurisdiction of the United States.

A scramble developed as to what would be done with territory comprising West Florida. When George Poindexter, Mississippi's territorial representative in Congress and later governor of Mississippi, took measures to add all of West Florida to the territory of Mississippi, he found opposition from Louisiana. A compromise resulted in the boundaries that now prevail, Mississippi getting all the territory from East Pearl River to St. Stephens Meridian, which is the Mississippi-Alabama line today. With the raising of the United States flag over this new territory, the stars and stripes joined four other flags, those raised by the French, Spanish, British, and West Florida. In 1861 the Bonnie Blue Flag of the Confederate States of America was unfurled, making six flags in all to fly over this area of South Mississippi. Other states, including South Carolina and Texas, had adopted this flag in various forms, with the background ranging from sky blue to navy, before Mississippi flew it in 1861. The Confederate Government never officially adopted it, in spite of its popularity among people in the South.

Even a brief history of the area that later became Pearl River County in the 1800s rivals anywhere else in the United States in its color and character. As General Andrew Jackson's army sought little-known passageways to transport artillery to New Orleans during the War of 1812, the Pearl River's proximity to the Gulf made it popular among pirates as well as the military. In 1814, Jackson was ordered to send his defense to the Mobile, Alabama area to defend New Orleans. Jackson's army crossed the (now) northern part of Pearl River County.

In 1872, Pearl River County was established originally as Pearl County, organized from parts of Hancock and Marion Counties. Riceville was the county seat and three commissioners were appointed by the governor to organize the county laws. Riceville's small, frame courthouse burned, destroying many of the records. Pearl County territory was returned to Hancock and Marion Counties and records made during the six years of its existence were deposited with the two older counties.

The Origin of Poplarville

In 1882, Poplarville was settled by "Poplar" Jim Smith, who traded ten bushels of corn for his claim of land. He built his first home where the Ruth Memorial Presbyterian Church now stands and his fields covered most of what is now the town of Poplarville. It is said that he built his home near a spring which flowed from under the roots of a large poplar tree, from which he earned the name "Poplar" Jim.

Byrd's Chapel was the original county seat. A Masonic Building was used to hold meetings. Soon after Byrd's Chapel was chosen to be the county seat, the Masonic building burned, and then the county seat was moved to Poplarville, which was centrally located. In 1892, after Poplarville became the county seat, Andrew Smith, son of "Poplar" Jim Smith, donated land to build a courthouse. The population of Poplarville at this time was 232, the largest town in Pearl River County.

When the county was re-created in 1890, Poplarville was made the county seat. Between 1890 and 1930, the population of Pearl River County grew from 2,957 to 19,405. The lumber industry dominated its economy, augmented by the production of turpentine and other naval stores. Farmers came to realize that the county's excellent grazing lands afforded good pasturage, and dairying and livestock raising became increasingly important. The sandy soil on the uplands were found to be adaptable to the cultivation of tung trees, the nuts from which valuable tung oil was produced.

Ox Teams in the Pearl River Swamp

Ox teams were an essential part of the chain in the settlement and development of south Mississippi, particularly in support of logging practices. As pine trees were felled, trimmed and

Logging with oxen in Pearl River swamp, early twentieth century.

cut into proper lengths, the logs were hauled to the nearest stream, rolled into the water and rafted for floating to the saw mill. Farmers found it profitable to raise and train oxen in teams to sell to the loggers for hauling the valuable timber. The driver and the oxen would work together as a highly trained team. They would walk up to their places and the yoke weighing about

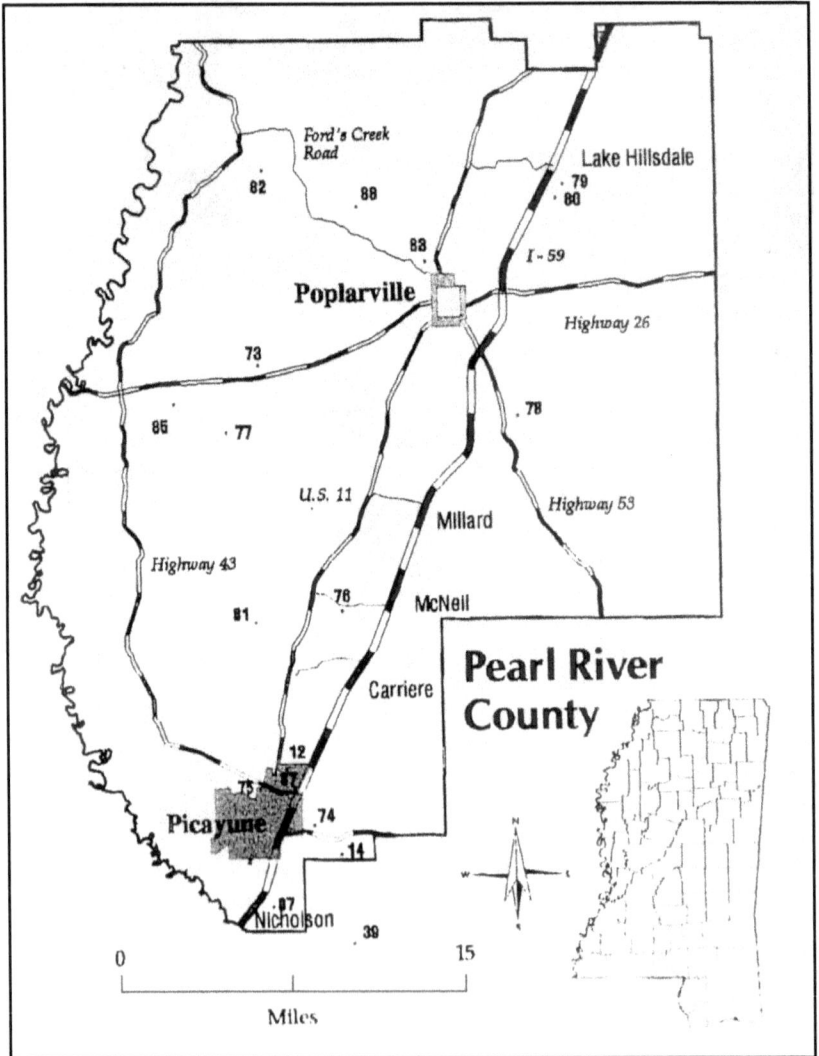

Poplarville, the heart of Pearl River County.

75 pounds would be placed over their necks with bows placed in the yoke, properly secured by pins. The teamwork was no less astonishing to bystanders when these beasts of burden responded to commands using their names, usually short and sweet, like Joe, Speck, or Spot.

The Country Doctor

In most communities, the country doctor had a special place in the hearts of the people. He was usually portrayed as ministering to the sick and suffering, without regard for money, but for the love of his fellow man. In the horse and buggy days, they went through mud and cold over impassable road conditions to visit the sick. If the distance were too much to run back and forth, the doctor would often stay at a home to watch until the crisis had passed. When it came time to pay, cash was a rarity; instead, the doctor was given the best of what the family could afford from their larder: fresh venison, homemade bread, new-crop peas.

Transportation

In the early 1900s, a trip across Pearl River County, from Bay St. Louis to Carriere, took about 12 hours on horseback.

Horses furnished the sole means of transportation away from the railway points and there was at least one livery stable in even the smallest of towns. Poplarville's location in the north central section of the county on U.S. Highway 11 was in a strategic geographical location along the New Orleans and Northeastern Railroad. The Pearl River Valley railroad ran between Nicholson and Rowlands in the western part of the county, while the Mississippi Southern Railroad covered the eastern portion.

In the 1800s, county residents must have been excited to hear a railroad was going to go through the center of the county, running north and south. Many people had never seen a train, much less ridden one. Later, in the 1900s, two Greyhound buses ran north and south each day, stopping in Poplarville at Ford's Cafe for meals.

The Grist Mill

Water as a power source played a significant role in the life of the rural southerner, from the baling of cotton to the processing of timber into lumber. Before rural families came to depend on the cotton gin and sawmill for their livelihood, however, the grist mill brought a quality of life to a community unlike any other mill site of the early days of the industrial age.

Today this kind of project would be built with dirt moving machines, but prior to mechanized labor, it took much manpower and time to complete the construction. Travelers from Savannah, Poplarville, Derby, McNeill, Leetown, Steep Hollow, and the Necaise area made it one of many stops, to get their corn ground while tending to other matters. Hot weather prohibited storing ground corn and the popularity of corn products in the South made the visits to the grist mill essential. A bushel of corn might take up to an hour to grind.

Also a staple for southerners at the turn of the century was the cane mill. No southern Mississippi pantry was complete without at least two of the products from the sugar cane crop: molasses and cane ribbon syrup. As recalled by those who lived during the popularity of the cane mill, October and November were known as molasses months, the best time to make this thick black syrup.

Hog-Killing

Another southern tradition that was related to a seasonal change was the practice of hog-killing and curing. Until the cold, wet weather of late fall or early winter arrived, it wasn't considered safe to process a hog for meat, due to the proliferation of parasites in the animal during warm weather months.

Most residents of the area not only raised their own meat animals, but butchered and cured the meat. Lack of refrigeration also prompted neighbors to cooperate by dividing up the cow or hog so it would be eaten before it spoiled. A large cast iron wash pot would be filled with water and a hot fire built under it. The hog was quickly killed, bled and put into boiling water. The hog would be hung up and left hanging for a time to cool off. Later, the hog would be cut into hams, back bones and other pieces. Other foods from hogs were cracklins and lard, used for cooking. Experienced cooks of this era (early 1900s) used pure lard for seasoning foods. The house on South St. Charles was a repository for the best of these southern foods—hogshead cheese, chitlins and sausage, biscuits and molasses—not only because Doc preferred these foods but because they were so accessible.

Piney Woods

The construction of sawmills which began in the early 1800's were the beginning of a major economic resource in South Mississippi. Mr. Ran Batson, president of Southern Lumber Company, had a large mill at Hillsdale. Doc was closely associated with Mr. Batson as a friend through the years. This part of the county's history I recall hearing about during my childhood years. Pearl River County began large scale exploitation of its virgin yellow pine just after the turn of the twentieth century. In 1929, 94,000 acres of timber remained in Pearl River County, but by 1993 tax rolls showed less than 33,000 and not more than 20,000 acres of this were virgin yellow pine. Pearl River County's high taxation policies caused this rapid decrease and small mills cleaned up what remained of the virgin pine after the large stands were gone.

The previously untapped virgin forests of the area lured large corporate investors to this region. The timber industry could not last forever and by 1930, many areas of the piney woods no longer contained the once plentiful long leaf pine. However, by the late 1940's, the efforts at reforestation began to pay dividends and the harvest of second growth pine forests once again brought economic opportunity to many South Mississippians. Firms such as Georgia Pacific, Masonite, and International Paper established sizable mills and brought forest lands once more to prominence within the region.

There were several saw mill companies operating in the country between 1906 and 1920. The mills produced about one million feet of lumber daily, accounting for about 2,000 acres of trees being cleared every month. Logs were carried by railway to Lumberton. Around Poplarville, mills sprang up in Orvisburg, Hillsdale, Dupont, Nortac, and Millard, places where Doc made house calls but some of which no longer appear on road maps.

The tung growing industry seemed to be the answer for Pearl River County's sterile, thin, acid soil. Little labor was required in tung growing except for spring cultivation and fall harvesting, which involved picking up the tung nuts. The United States had no other sure source of tung oil, which was used in high-quality paints and varnishes. In September of 1937, *National Geographic Magazine* featured Mississippi with an article titled "You Plant a Tung Tree Then Wait for the Nuts to Fall." More than half of the tung trees then in the United States were grown in Pearl River County. Ironically, this issue of *National Geographic* appeared soon after Japan had invaded China and effectively cut off exports to the Yangtze River valley for over eight years, just as the American groves along the Gulf Coast were ready to produce.

The Telephone

Early in 1903, the first telephone system in Poplarville was operating, and by 1906, a telephone line connected Orvisburg, Hillsdale, McNeill, and Carriere, with just one telephone in each town. In 1912, the Southern Bell Telephone and Telegraph Company bought almost the entire stock of the Cumberland Telephone and Telegraph Company. In 1926, these two companies merged. Telephone numbers in the days of Doc's early practice were easy to remember; his office number was 89 and his home number was 35.

Poplarville Chamber of Commerce

In 1937, a meeting was set to organize the Chamber of Commerce in Poplarville. The following officers were elected to head the organization: Mayor Dwight L. Wesley, President, and J. R. Roberts, Secretary and Treasurer. Board of Directors: W. B.

Williams, J. B. Mayfield, Ellis Mitchell, C. G Hartzog, D. B. Davis, G. L. Spotswood, and C. Provost.

Newspapers

The Poplarville Sun was published in Poplarville in 1888. In 1889, *The Poplarville Enterprise* was published for about eight months. When Pearl River County was established in 1890, Lumberton was included in the county and *The Lumberton Headbloc* was the county newspaper. In 1904, Lumberton was included in Lamar County. *The Free Press* was published beginning in 1891 in Poplarville and eventually took the place of *The Lumberton Headbloc*. Picayune was admitted to Pearl River County in 1900 and *The Picayune Item* came on the scene in 1904. In 1933, *The Democrat* was published in Poplarville, eventually taking the place of *The Free Press*. This newspaper, known first as *The Weekly Democrat*, is now published as *The Poplarville Democrat*.

Poplarville Today

The location of Poplarville affords the area with an excellent access to transportation. Located at the intersection of Highways 11 and 26, (and Interstate 59) it is on the New Orleans and Northeastern division of the Southern Railway. Being only 75 miles from the port at New Orleans and 52 miles from the Gulfport port, this strategic location gives transportation outlet to big market centers of New Orleans, the Gulf Coast, Baton Rouge, Mobile, and Hattiesburg. Since Poplarville is the county seat of Pearl River County and located in the center of the tung, timber and cattle belt of South Mississippi, it holds out many opportunities to the industrial or agricultural minded investor.

The 1960 Census reported the population of Poplarville as 2,134 and the Pearl River County population as 22,411. This population showed a rapid rise due to the construction activity in the establishment of the NASA test site in the area adjacent to

Pearl River County. Today, several U.S. science, naval, and space technology agencies operate major facilities in or near Pearl River County, employing thousands of people. According to the Mississippi Development Authority, the population of Poplarville was 2,601 in 2000, while Pearl River County had a population of 48,621 in the same year.

In 1994, students from the sixth-grade class of Poplarville Upper Elementary School were sent on mission to learn all they could about the formation and early life of Pearl River County. The result is their one-of-a-kind collection of stories titled *Pearl River County: 100 Years Ago.* Sydney Woodson wrote about Theodore Gilmore Bilbo being elected to the Mississippi Senate in 1907 and later being elected governor twice, then serving in the United States Senate. Sydney recalls his mother referring to Governor Bilbo as a presence in the Federal building in Jackson where she used to work, that "she used to hear doors slam late at night and footsteps in the hallways. Everyone claimed it was Bilbo's ghost!" Another student, Hank Shackelford, interviewed Miss Virginia McCants, who was a good friend of the Cowart family as well as secretary to attorney Hubert Parker. She told young Hank that long ago the streets of Poplarville were not paved or covered with gravel but by oyster shells. This collection of anecdotal stories is a treasure not only because it reveals some long-forgotten facts about Poplarville, but it is also a remarkable effort in language arts by elementary school students.

Pearl River Community College

On July 7, 1909, three thousand people were present to witness the cornerstone laying for the new Agricultural High School building and to enjoy the barbecue on the campus of the Poplarville High School, which had been in existence for some time. Early in the morning the crowd began to gather from all directions, hundreds of people were reported to be coming in on the regularly scheduled train. On Tuesday, September 6, 1910, the Agricultural High School opened its second session with five faculty and one administrator. The boys were taught farming while the girls were taught cooking, sewing and other arts of housework. In 1911 the junior college building was added, giving the school increased facilities which put it in a category by itself. The same year the enrollment reached 250, with representatives from twenty-five counties.

On September 7, 1926, Pearl River Junior College had its formal opening ceremony, making it the oldest two-year institution in the state, the oldest in the gulf south, second oldest in the deep south and the thirty-first organized in the nation.

In 1953, Dr. Garvin H. Johnston was appointed President of the College by the Board of Trustees. Coming out of the Great Depression, most students had to earn their way through junior colleges; Garvin Johnston was no exception. By his own admission, he had to borrow five cents from his professor to buy his first pencil. The junior college severed its direct relations with the high school in the spring of 1960. In the fall of that year, the eleventh and twelfth grades were taught in a new senior high school building. At this time, they came under the supervision of the superintendent of the Poplarville City School System. Dr. Johnston's role in education did not end here. In August 1967, former PRC President Johnston became Mississippi Superintendent of Education.

On October 12, 1967, Dr. Marvin R. White was elected president of Pearl River Junior College to succeed Dr. Johnston. Dr. White, who was Dean of the College at the time, officially took office on January 15, 1968. Dr. Ted Alexander was President of the College from 1986-2000, after it became known as Pearl River Community College. Since 2000, Dr. William Lewis has filled the role of President of the College.

Doc was the Pearl River College physician from about 1930 until the mid 1950s, inspiring our family's involvement in Pearl River Community College's growth and activities. We were always attending the PRC ball games, enjoying Coach Dobie Holden's winning Wildcat football team. My memories of faculty and staff at this college are incomplete without mention of typing in Mrs. Elnora Holden' class, or being enthralled by a retelling of a true event in the life of Huey P. Long in one of Mr. Enoch Seal's history classes. And of course, I owe much of my knowledge of high school geometry to Mr. Marvin White, who had no equal when it came to teaching mathematics, and who encouraged excellence from students in much the same way when he became Dr. White, President of the College. Names like Miss Dixie Clanton and Miss Eunice McSwain bring to mind the good old days of the Fifties for me, as much as the sense of community around the grist mill did for a previous generation.

Salute to Poplarville

From my vantage point, Poplarville was the best small town in the world in which to grow up. Having Doc for my grandfather was a bigger than life experience for me. We didn't have many dull moments. There were so many wonderful people in Poplarville and most of my experiences were pleasant from my birth through the time when I left home to go away to college. The memories which I continue to associate with Poplarville are invaluable. I love going back to visit with friends and family. These good times are indeed treasures. Kathryn Moody captured the heart and history of Pearl River County in fine verse:

Rivers—In General

Long ago a Hand grasped the earth to put it on course,
gain harmony and be a place for man.
Where the fingers pressed hardest became rivers of water
to lace the greenness of the rest of it,
bordering or dividing, but
always plunging toward some sea.
She gathers into her far-flung arms
the water running from hillside streams,
big and bold (always bigger when we are young).

Pearl River—Particularly

It is said that DeSoto found his way up this river
to a vantage point high and overlooking.
Today we put a cornerstone there . . . for opening later.
Pearl River, with time carving through the south of Mississippi,
leaving a trail through history and hearts,
becoming the boundary of so much of our lives,
the source of political debate.

But the River herself:
Relentless, yet lingering to ebb and flow and pool
a deep mystery with a serene and beautiful curling surface,
surging toward some goal she has set for herself.
She accepts offerings from the streams pouring their allotted volumes
into the silent sidewater . . .
We can watch as the sun sets into motion
thousands of frantic golden sparkles,
each bounding higher than the other,
reflecting light and giving it to us on a silver platter of stillness.
We can only dream about what is upriver along the banks . . .
One thing we know, as this river swings her arms into the fertile
deltas along her way, we can count the loss of oak and cypress trees
one at a time.
Doesn't she care that she is gradually taking us all with her?
We find a long stretch of sand, sit and watch
to get a glimpse of some secret she is keeping from us
until she is ready.
The fish share her secrets,
the alligators seldom want to leave the sanctity of her belly.
The night birds call to each other across her banks
as the cypress trees gnarl up on knobby knees to bow down
in her presence . . .
There is a bluff that is awesome;
she just could not reach that high
when she is pulling in her skirts for the trip down river.
She has, frivolously, spread sand along strips of bank . . .
as if it were wedding veil to dry. Overhanging tree branches
cradle sentinel snakes lying contoured with the limb.
The River greets us sometimes with the nod of a wave,
at times tumultuous—or graceful and polite.
The tornadic labor of Spring finally delivers great, rolling
waves plunging headlong toward the gulf.
We are reminded of power.
After a Winter of plodding along and pausing to rest,
she has gained strength and reserve
for the time when people will come
to build and stay or visit and dream.
Human beings, historically, struggle to own a spot of land

along the rim of the River;
somehow to become a part of the constancy
to experience endurance,
to become the same yesterday, tomorrow and today . . .
Or, to feel the life force of nature
harmonizing with the countryside we're lucky enough to call home.

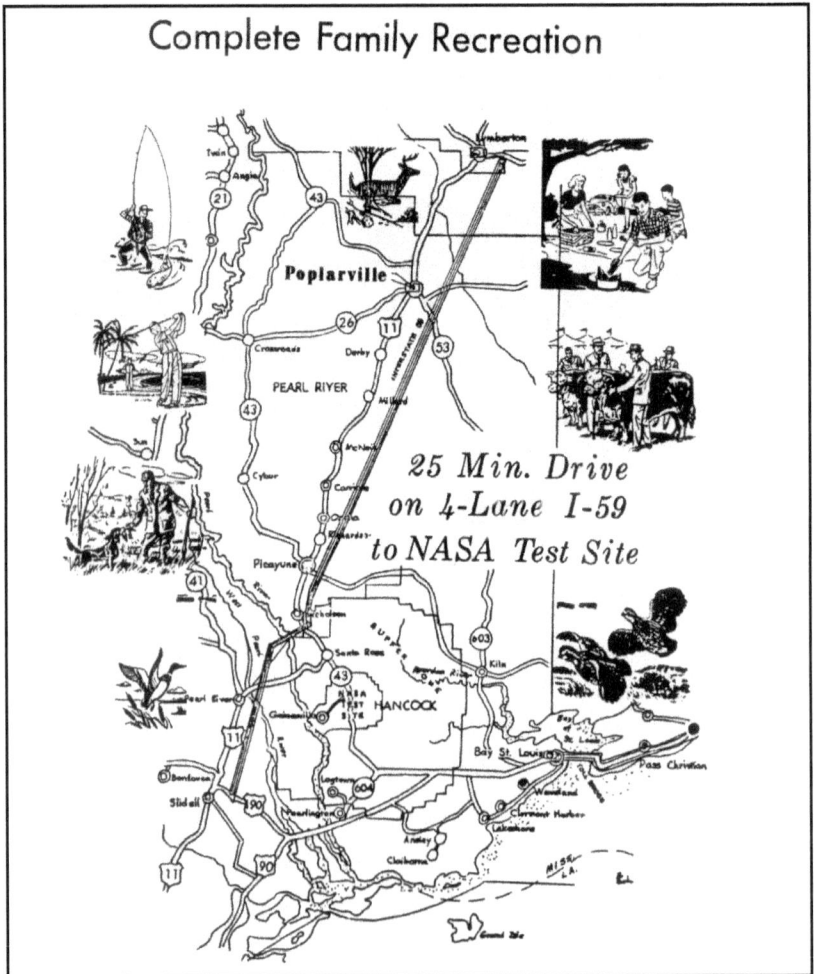

An early promotion of the NASA test site, which brought jobs to thousands in Pearl River County.

Ted J. Alexander Building. The two-story, 22,000 square foot administration building was renovated and expanded in 1999 from a single story, 7,735 square foot structure built in 1963.

—Picture courtesy of Pearl River Community College, Poplarville, Mississippi.

Jane and Frank Brister on the Ole Miss campus, 1960.

Epilogue

The wine of life is drawn, and the mere lees is left this vault to brag of.
William Shakespeare, from Macbeth, Act II, Scene III

lees (noun): the sediment of a liquor (as wine) during fermentation and aging.
Merriam-Webster Dictionary (www.m-w.com/cgi-bin/dictionary)

When Frank and I were in graduate school at The University of Mississippi in Oxford, Doc had been very supportive of what we were doing, as well as of Ole Miss. After I graduated in 1961, we were on our way to Poplarville and stopped to visit my grandfather, who was in the Hattiesburg hospital for some tests. I showed him my degree and he was so proud that he left the hospital without even checking out and drove himself home. On that occasion, I was basking in his praise, but I also remember his wit and wisdom. He said that the doctor in charge asked him how he had maintained such a young man's heart at age eighty. He replied, "I know how to space my whiskey." His implied reference to moderation in lifestyle has never left me.

When Maudie had her first heart attack in 1962, I was married and living in Jackson, Mississippi. Kathryn Moody called me and told me that earlier that day Maudie had had a hard coronary and she thought I should come. I went to Poplarville as soon as I could drive down there and remember Bigum saying, "The Good Lord sent her down here." After we went home from the hospital that evening, we sat down in the middle of the big

131

bedroom, where we always visited. Bigum told us Maudie had some complications and it had been his experience in her particular case that she would have another attack within 24 hours and it would take her. That is exactly what happened.

In the late 1960s, Bigum retired and, probably because he could no longer do the thing he loved most in the world, began a decline that would eventually land him in a nursing facility. Before he left the Poplarville hospital to enter the Hattiesburg nursing home, I heard Bigum say he had "lived life to the lees."

He had as few regrets as any on a professional level; the only regret he had personally was that he would have his own airplane, if he had it to over again. The times and seasons with Doc seem like yesterday. Recalling them reminds me that he was a dominant figure in my life and my heart. When he passed away, it was difficult for me to grasp the reality that someone who had so much life in him could actually be dead. It was too much to process at the time. At some point, he had requested that the church organist, Mrs. Joyce Mitchell, play "It is Well With My Soul" at his funeral, which she did, and played it well. He was a member of First Baptist Church but somehow I always felt he was one of the best Methodists I ever knew. I think much of the stuff that made up his personality can be summed up in the words of one of his favorite songs, "I Believe":

> I believe for every drop of rain that falls, a flower grows.
> I believe that somewhere in the darkest night, a candle glows.
> I believe for everyone who goes astray,
> Someone will come to show the way.
> I believe, I believe.
> I believe above the storm the smallest pray'r will still be heard.
> I believe that someone in the great somewhere hears every word.
> Every time I hear a newborn baby cry,
> Or touch a leaf, or see the sky,
> Then I know why I believe.

When I met my husband during my junior year at Mississippi College, he encouraged me to get in touch with my father through Alumni records from Columbia University in New York. I did just that and the result was very rewarding. My father and I corresponded from that time on and he visited me on several occasions.

It was as though we picked up where we left off years ago. This is probably the best place to finish this part of the story.

After Doc's death in 1970, when my husband, Frank, and our two young sons were living in Brownwood, Texas, an interesting thing happened. Grandaddy Ross (as he was later referred to by my family), called to tell me that his wife had died, and after this, the rest of the story is still hard to believe. He and my mother began corresponding again and he called her everyday for about six months. They eventually remarried and each sold their homes, in Maryland and Poplarville, and moved to Newhebron, Mississsippi where my grandmother's relatives lived. They had about twelve years together before he died in 1982 and her death in 1983. They visited us in Texas several times and we did some special things together as a family.

It seems almost mystical that my parents, Louise and Ross Marshall, were reconciled after my own family and I moved to Texas in the early 1970s. With so many stories to tell, this book seemed inevitable. My two young sons became acquainted with their grandparents as a couple after they were married for the second time. We enjoyed over a decade of good times together.

Life's little rites of passage come with much wonderment and reflection. So many moments of everyday memories become more and more precious as time moves forward. Looking back is a privilege and sometimes an awe-inspiring thing to recall the fleeting days of yesteryear. Writing this book has been a worthwhile challenge and the time has been right for the reliving of the Poplarville era with my grandfather, Dr. H. B. Cowart. These special times are more revered than ever after spreading all these experiences out on the dining room table, while putting the pieces together.

Life's ebb and flow has certainly had a mesmerizing effect on my dance with destiny. As a small portion of history has been retold, we all seem to have found our place in the sun, like Doc. For the dear departed who could have contributed so much to the stories in this book, God rest your souls. For those who are still living the journey on this earth and who contributed to the narrative, you have my heartfelt gratitude. Many people have said that Doc would be so pleased with this tribute to him.

Thank you, Bigum, for a lifetime of priceless memories.

Ross and Louise Marshall, Poplarville, Mississippi (c. 1935).

Mama Ease (Louise Cowart Marshall) and Granddaddy Ross (Ross Marshall), au-thor's parents (c. 1980).

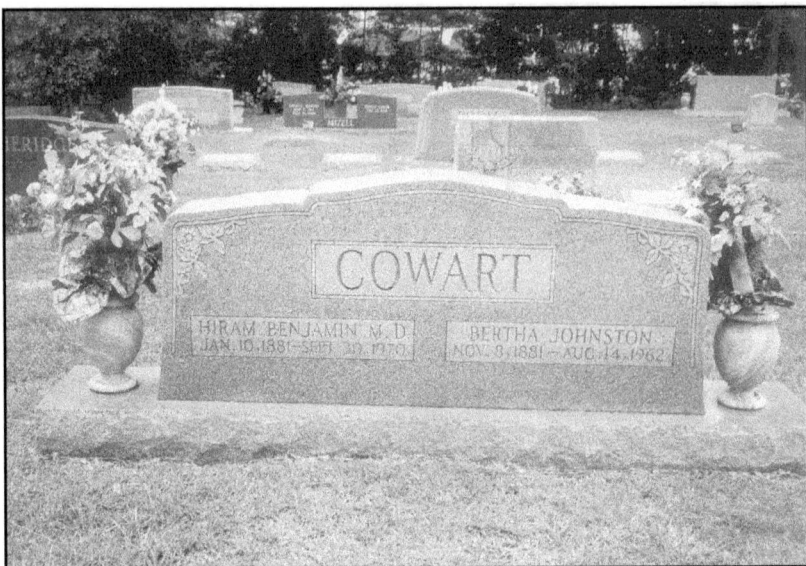

Doc and Maudie's final resting place, Poplarville, Mississippi.

*Dr. H. B. Cowart
(c. 1940s).*

Selected Bibliography

Archival Collections

Hattiesburg.   University of Southern Mississippi Library. The Historical Records Survey.

Hattiesburg.   University of Southern Mississippi McCain Library. Timber Related Source Materials About Mississippi's Piney Woods.

Jackson.   Mississippi Department of Archives and History: Cemetery Records of Lawrence County. Monticello Masonic Cemetery Records. Blue Book Biennial Report. Mississippi Official and Statistical Register.

Jackson.   Mississippi Development Authority.

Jackson.   State Department of Agriculture. Bulletin Report of Agricultural Products of Mississippi in 1936.

Jackson.   The Mississippi Library Commission.

Books

Anderson, Peggy (compiler). *Great Quotes from Great Leaders.* Lombard, IL: Celebrating Excellence Publishing, 1990.

Beck, Roger, et al. *Modern World History Patterns of Interaction.* "Global Impact Influenza Epidemic." Evanston, IL: McDougal Littell, 1999.

Clay, Floyd Martin. Coozan Ludley Leblanc: From Huey Long to Hadacol. Monticello, KY: Firebird Press, 1987.

Dorland, W. A. Newman (ed.). *Dorland's Illustrated Medical Dictionary* (25th ed.). Philadelphia: W. B. Saunders Company, 1974.

Foner, Eric & John A. Garraty (eds.). *The Reader's Companion to American History.* New York: Houghton Mifflin Company, 1991.

Frost-Knappman, Elizabeth (ed.). *The World Almanac of Presidential Quotations: Quotations from America's Presidents.* New York: Pharos Books, 1988.

Maggio, Rosalie (compiler). *The Beacon Book of Quotations by Women*. Boston: Beacon Press, 1992.

Merck's 1899 Manual. New York: Merck and Company.

Napier, John Hawkins, III. *Lower Pearl River's Pineywoods: Its Land and People*. Oxford: The University of Mississippi Center for the Study of Southern Culture, 1985.

New Encyclopaedia Britannica. Macropaedia, Vol. 18. Chicago: Encyclopaedia Britannica, Inc., 1974.

Thigpen, S. J. *Highway to Glory Land*. Kingsport, TN: Kingsport Press, Inc. 1965.

Thigpen, S. J. *Next Door to Heaven*. Kingsport, TN: Kingsport Press, Inc., 1965.

Turner, Richard B. *Once Upon a Country Doctor*. San Francisco: Sonrise, 1994.

Webster's Third New International Dictionary, 9th unabridged. Springfield, MA: G & C Merriam Company, 1966.

Internet Sources

"A Selected Cowpie Song." www.roughstock.com/cowpie/songs/

"The Sting That Heals." www.beelief.com/beestings.html

"The Thomsonian System." www.rt66.com/hrbmoore/ManualsOther/Colby-1.txt

"Yorklyn Timeline." www.delawareonline.com/newsjournal/local/2002/02/02yorklyn_timeline.html.

Newspapers

The Battle Cry (United Daughters of the Confederacy Newspaper)

The Clarion Ledger

The Commercial Appeal

The Hattiesburg American

The Pearl River Countan

The Poplarville Democrat (formerly *The Weekly Democrat*)

The Simpson County News

The Times-Picayune

The Tupelo Journal

Other Records

Drake, Ervin, I. Graham, J. Shirl, & A. Stillman. *I Believe* [sheet music]. New York: Cromwell Music, Inc., 1952.

"Pearl River County—100 Years Ago." Collection of stories written by sixth-grade students. Poplarville Upper Elementary School Class of 2000.

Wallace, Diana. "The History of Poplarville." Term paper by Poplarville High School student, 2002.

About the Author

Jane Elizabeth Marshall Brister was born in 1937 in Poplarville, Mississippi, delivered by her grandfather, Dr. H. B. Cowart. She lived with her mother, Lola Louise Cowart Marshall, and her grandparents, Dr. and Mrs. Cowart, until she left Poplarville to attend Mississippi College in Clinton, Mississippi. After receiving a B.A. in 1959, she married Frank L. Brister, Jr., from Yazoo City, Mississippi, who is now a professor at Stephen F. Austin State University in Nacogdoches, Texas. Jane and Frank currently reside in Nacogdoches and have two sons, Frank III and Ben, and five grandchildren.

In 1960 Jane was named to the *World Who's Who of Women* and in 1961 she received her Master of Education from The University of Mississippi in Oxford, Mississippi. In 1972 she was named among *Outstanding Young Women of America*. She was also selected to appear in the 1976-77 edition of *Personalities of the South,* in recognition of achievements and outstanding service to community and state. After serving Mississippi and Texas public

schools as a teacher and counselor for thirty years, Jane retired in 1993. In addition to being a member of the Daughters of the American Revolution, the Order of the First Families of Mississippi, the United Daughters of the Confederacy, and University Women, Jane is a member of the Westminster Presbyterian Church handbell choir and has served as an Elder on several committees. She enjoys writing, playing the piano, and especially cherishes spending time with her grandchildren.

Jane's first-hand perspective of her grandfather's medical practice, from the 1940s until his retirement in 1965, inspired her to tell his story. She believed these efforts have provided a legacy not only for Dr. Cowart's descendants, but also for a generation that can only imagine the way things were when Doc was practicing medicine.

www.ingramcontent.com/pod-product-compliance
Lightning Source LLC
Chambersburg PA
CBHW070332090426
42733CB00012B/2448